EVERYTHING

JESUS

PURCHASED

FOR YOU

Everything Jesus Purchased for You

First Edition, First Impression 2019

Copyright © Pastor Gerald Hugo

Contact Information:
www.gracetabernaclechurch.co.za
www.geraldhugo.com.
Telephone: +27 63 780 4526

Editing and proofreading by Ronell Swartz
Cover design by: Pearl Motloutsi
Layout design and typesetting by: Saqib Arshad

ISBN: 978-0-620-92782-6

Scripture References

Scripture quotations marked AMP are from the Amplified Bible. Copyright © 1954, 1958, 1962, 1964, 1965, 1987 by The Lockman Foundation. All rights reserved. Used by permission.

Scripture quotations marked KJV are from the King James Version of the Bible.

Scripture quotations marked MSG are taken from The Message. Copyright 1993, 1994, 1995, 1996, 2000, 2001, 2002. Used by permission of NavPress Publishing Group.

Scripture quotations marked NIV are from the New International Version of the Bible. Copyright © 1973, 1978, 1984, 2011 by International Bible Study Society. Used by permission. All rights reserved.

Scripture quotations marked NKJV are from the New King James Version of the Bible. Copyright © 1982 by Thomas Nelson, Inc. Used by permission. All rights reserved.

PASTOR GERALD HUGO

EVERYTHING JESUS PURCHASED FOR YOU

Discover your benefits of the Finished works of The Cross

DEDICATION

I dedicate this book to my wife Innes Hugo and my children Javen, Yanez and Chay who sacrificed our time together for me to write this book. Javen would ask me so often, "Is daddy busy writing another book?" "Yes, my son, this is it."

I thank the Grace Tabernacle Church family and my Office staff whose dedication and sacrifices know no limit. Your hunger for the truth provoked my anointing to pen down the wisdom of God and to make it plain so a herald can run with it.

I also dedicate this book to those who are hungry for the Word of God; those who are done with spiritual entertainment and charismatic coaching. May this book cause you to have a clear understanding of the word of God and have a closer walk with Jesus.

ABOUT THE AUTHOR

Pastor Gerald Hugo is the senior pastor and founder of Grace Tabernacle Church with the head office in Mamelodi, Pretoria, South Africa, and branches in other provinces.

Pastor Hugo preaches the Gospel of the Kingdom of God with signs following. He is the visionary of *The 2020 Mandate* and the custodian of *Beyond 2020 Projects*. His messages and teachings empower the hearer, thus their lives are totally transformed for the better, through the working of the Holy Spirit. People from all walks of life are travelling on a weekly basis, some as far as 200 kilometres, to come and listen to him preaching the Gospel without compromise, fear or favour.

Pastor Hugo had various one-on-one encounters with God, and on 16 December 1996 he was also raised from the dead. When asked if he thinks these spiritual encounters hold any significance in the success of his ministry, he says, "I am what I am only by the grace of God."

More information about Pastor Gerald Hugo and his ministry is available at:
www.gracetabernaclechurch.co.za
www.geraldhugo.com

CONTENTS

CHAPTER 1

THE FINISHED WORK OF THE CROSS

John 17:4

[4] I have glorified You on the earth. I have finished the work which You have given Me to do.

The work of Jesus

The coming of Jesus to the earth was for a specific assignment. Jesus had a work to do. At the end of His journey on earth, Jesus told the Father that He had finished the work the Father had sent Him to do. His last words on the cross were also, *"It is finished."* With these words Jesus hung His head and died. The question is: What was finished? What was the work of Jesus? Why did He come to the earth? What did He accomplish?

The works that Jesus finished on the cross

- He took away Sin
- He brought us Grace
- He paid for our Healing
- He delivered us from Demonic Oppression
- He made us Righteous
- He made us Rich
- He gave us Peace
- He gave us Eternal Life
- He gave us the Holy Spirit

He took away our Sin

John 1:29
[29] The next day John saw Jesus coming toward him, and said, "Behold! The Lamb of God who takes away the sin of the world!"

Jesus came to take away the sins of the world. Everybody's past, present and future sin is forgiven. This verse can give rise to the following three questions: if God has forgiven my past, present and future sin, can I continue to live in sin and still go to heaven? Why would God send people to hell after Jesus paid for their sin? If God is so good, why does He send people to hell? The answer to all these questions is this: God has made provision for everybody to go to heaven, by sending His son to pay for the penalty of sin. The death of Jesus has made provision for us to let go of sin and receive salvation, therefore we should not continue to live in sin.

God will send nobody to hell; He has sent Jesus to take us all to heaven, but those who prefer not to receive the salvation God has provided, will go to hell out of their own decision and not by the will of God. After God had created all mankind, He still gave each person the privilege of choice to decide whether we want Him or the devil. That is love beyond limits. Everybody's sin is paid for, but everybody has to receive the forgiveness of their sin through salvation. If a person prefers not to receive salvation, they have indirectly chosen hell as their destination.

Be aware that the sins of the world were indeed paid for in full by the death of Jesus, but every man still has to receive salvation through the name of Jesus Christ in order to go to heaven. Guard against the doctrine of inclusivity that suggests that no matter how much you sin, everybody is going to heaven at the end. Be aware, there are mainstream television shows and movies out there by once prominent Pentecostals that suggest that everybody is going to heaven, because Jesus already paid for their sin. That is not what I am propagating with this point. If everybody is going to heaven then why did Jesus tell Nicodemus that he must be born again to enter the kingdom of heaven? Why did Jesus instruct the disciples to make disciples of all nations? Study the word of God so you will not be easily mislead by false doctrines. No matter how much you sin, God still loves you, but it does not mean you will go to heaven if the Lord returns suddenly, or if you suffer sudden death before repentance. You must be born again.

He brought us Grace

Through His death, Jesus came to usher in the Grace of God. He fulfilled the requirements of The Law and He brought in Grace. We are no longer under the Law but under Grace.

Romans 10:4 NKJV
[4] For Christ is the end of the law for righteousness to everyone who believes.

Through the Grace of God your past, present and future sins are forgiven. You can have boldness when you approach the throne of Grace to receive answers to all your prayers. The devil can no longer condemn you, *"For there is therefore now no condemnation for those who are in Christ Jesus."* Grace is not a licence to sin but a gift of empowerment that boosts your faith to believe God for anything.

He paid for our Healing

1 Peter 2:24
[24] who Himself bore our sins in His own body on the tree, that we, having died to sins, might live for righteousness--by whose stripes you were healed.

According to our Lord Jesus Christ, we are already healed. No Christian is supposed to be sick. Healing is an inheritance of the child of God because of Jesus who died as the testator of the will of God. You have to receive your healing by Grace through Faith. You don't have to work for your healing; you have to believe for it. You can claim your healing by grace through faith. Cast out any form of sickness with great authority. If you are sick just say, "Thank You Lord. I receive my healing Jesus has already paid for. I am healed." From then on declare you are healed. Speak and believe it against all odds. Study the word of God further concerning the subject of healing and believe the report of the Lord.

He delivered us from Demonic Oppression

The subject of deliverance is a very controversial subject in the church of the Lord Jesus Christ. With deliverance we refer here to deliverance from demonic possession or oppression. There are those who believe that a Christian can be demon possessed. I disagree with that belief because it is unscriptural. God is light and in Him there is no darkness at all. He whom the son sets free is free indeed. God will not share the same room with the devil. A person cannot have both God and the devil in their spirit. Light and darkness cannot share the same room. The minute light comes in, darkness flees at the speed of light. If the one is in, the other is out.

Secondly, the Greek word for the word salvation is *soteria,* which means to deliver, to save, to preserve and to redeem. When a person receives salvation, they have received deliverance.

What I do agree with is that a Christian can be demon oppressed. The person might have Christ on the inside and be oppressed by demons from the outside. The minute a Christian is possessed by the devil they are no longer a Christian. In the following verse we see that God has indeed delivered us from the kingdom of darkness.

Colossians 1:13 NKJV
[13] *He has delivered us from the power of darkness and conveyed us into the kingdom of the Son of His love.*

He made us Righteous

Through the death of Jesus Christ, we have received righteousness as a gift and not a reward for good works.

2 Corinthians 5:21 KJV
[21] *For he hath made him to be sin for us, who knew no sin; that we might be made the righteousness of God in him.*

We were made the righteousness of God in Christ. You are not going to become or going to be made righteous; you are righteous. You are in right standing with God this very moment. You can ask anything from God and He will give it to you.

He made us Rich

2 Corinthians 8:9
[9] *For you know the grace of our Lord Jesus Christ, that though He was rich, yet for your sakes He became poor, that you through His poverty might become rich.*

As a child of God you are rich, irrespective of your bank balance. You might be temporarily out of cash, but you are not poor. You are rich. Believe it and keep speaking it. Let money and divine ideas to produce wealth come to you.

He gave us Peace

Peace is the most precious gift on the earth. Freedom fighters have spent years in prison to fight for peace. Wars are fought in countries to obtain peace. Peace in this world does not last. Many countries have fought for peace and equality and some have reduced their once prosperous countries to a heap of ruins and economic desperation. In the verse below, Jesus tells us He does not give peace like the world does; He gives true peace that is eternal.

I have heard people say to me many times, "Pastor, I don't want money, a car or a new house, I just want peace." You may have a mansion with a comfortable bed, but if you don't have peace, a person in a shack can have a better quality of sleep than you.

John 14:27 NKJV
[27] Peace I leave with you, My peace I give to you; not as the world gives do I give to you. Let not your heart be troubled, neither let it be afraid.

Take a moment right now and receive the peace of God into your spirit. It is about time you have eternal peace. A sleep-inducing pill might put you to sleep but it cannot give you peace. Jesus has eternal peace for you. Just receive by grace through faith.

He gave us Eternal Life

Eternal life is the life of God at work in an ordinary human being. It is that life that raised Jesus from the dead. *"The same spirit that raised Jesus from death is in you and it will give life to your mortal body"* **(Romans 8:11).** When you are facing any sickness or infirmity in your body, the eternal life of God that is at work in you will revive (quicken, resurrect, revitalise) your mortal body.

Eternal life will also cause you to live even after you have died. Those who die without Christ will return to the dust never to see the light of day again **(Psalm 49:19).**

John 3:16
[16] For God so loved the world, that he gave his only begotten Son, that whosoever believeth in him should not perish, but have everlasting life.

He gave us the Holy Spirit

The Holy Spirit is the mighty third person of the trinity. He is the indwelling Christ. He is Jesus with unlimited power and ability. Through the Holy Spirit Jesus is no longer confined to one place. He can be everywhere, where His people are. If people are looking for Jesus on the earth, they can see Jesus who is now in you. You can do the same miracles Jesus did by the Power of the Holy Spirit who is at work in you. Jesus died and went to heaven for our advantage; so we can have the Holy Spirit which is the same power by which He did miracles. It is the same power that kept Him alive and which He blew out on the cross and died. It is the same power which returned and resurrected Him back to life. That power is now at work in you and me.

John 16:7
[7] Nevertheless I tell you the truth. It is to your advantage that I go away; for if I do not go away, the Helper will not come to you; but if I depart, I will send Him to you.

It is finished

I want you to pay special attention to the highlighted portion of the scripture below. These were the last moments and the last words of Jesus on the cross.

John 19:28-30 KJV
*[28] After this, **Jesus knowing that all things were now accomplished,** that the scripture might be fulfilled, saith, I thirst. [29] Now there was set a vessel full of vinegar: and they filled a spunge with vinegar, and put it upon hyssop, and put it to his mouth.*

*[30] When Jesus therefore had received the vinegar, **he said, It is finished**: and he bowed his head, and gave up the ghost.*

Have you noticed that the minute Jesus knew He had finished His assignment He said, "It is finished," and then He died? Jesus left nothing undone. There is nothing you can add to complete your healing, deliverance, salvation, righteousness, peace, wealth, eternal life, grace and the Holy Spirit in your life. Jesus paid it in full.

It is finished!

CHAPTER 2

WHAT IS SALVATION?

When someone claims to be saved, the question then is, what are you saved from? Most people's understanding of salvation is that they are saved from sin. We are not only saved from sin, but we are saved from satan. Sin is one of the things satan brings into a person's life. Sickness, oppression, demonic possession, poverty, discouragement, depression and fear are all things that come from satan. When you got saved, you were saved from everything that satan can bring into a person's life.

The meaning of the word *Salvation*

According to Strong's Concordance, the word *salvation* is *soteria* in the Greek and it means deliverance, preservation, safety, redemption and salvation. To see salvation only as the deliverance from sin is a total misunderstanding of what Jesus came to do for us.

Pastor Gerald Hugo

The major things Salvation includes

- Preservation (to be saved from sin)
- Protection
- Deliverance
- Healing
- Provision

Preservation

Matthew 1:21 NKJV
[21] And she will bring forth a Son, and you shall call His name JESUS, for He will save His people from their sins.

To preserve something means to keep it safe; to keep it from being wasted or destroyed. It's like when you take money and put it away; you will say I am saving the money. What you mean is that you keep it from being wasted and you place it in a safe place. It is not beneficial to live in sin, therefore God sent Jesus to save us from sin.

The very sin that man commits is destroying him. God has saved us from destroying ourselves with sin. Jesus came to save us from self-destruction. Through sin a man is busy destroying himself. Think about it for a minute; what are the consequences of for instance smoking and drinking? Smoking tobacco destroys your lungs and drinking alcohol destroys your liver.

Saved from addiction

Romans 6:17-23 NKJV
[17] But God be thanked that though you were slaves of sin, yet you obeyed from the heart that form of doctrine to which you were delivered. [18] And having been set free from sin, you became slaves of righteousness. [19] I speak in human terms because of the weakness of your flesh. For just as you presented your members as slaves of uncleanness, and of lawlessness leading to more

lawlessness, so now present your members as slaves of righteousness for holiness. [20] For when you were slaves of sin, you were free in regard to righteousness. [21] What fruit did you have then in the things of which you are now ashamed? For the end of those things is death. [22] But now, having been set free from sin, and having become slaves of God, you have your fruit to holiness, and the end, everlasting life. [23] For the wages of sin is death, but the gift of God is eternal life in Christ Jesus our Lord.

Most sins lead to addiction and ultimately destruction. Paul says we were slaves to sin. The word *slave* in this context refers to addiction, which means that someone who sins has a tendency to become addicted to the act of sinning. It is this very reason why many people find it hard to receive salvation. They know they should be saved; they know they are doing wrong; they know they are on their way to hell by committing sin; and they want to be right with God, but their addiction to sin keeps them from receiving salvation.

They know smoking is destroying their lungs. Those who consume alcohol know alcohol is deadly; they know it is poisonous, but they still consume it. That is what is called an addiction.

A person may say, "I am not an addict." Then stop what you are doing. The key is if you are not addicted to something you will be able to put a stop to it immediately at will. If you can't, you are addicted. You may say, "I only drink once in a while." Then, if you are not addicted, stop drinking once in a while. If you can't, you are addicted. Every addiction starts with small engagements and it gradually builds up.

Protection

Proverbs 18:10 NKJV
[10] The name of the LORD is a strong tower; the righteous run to it and are safe.

God's Name is our protection. As believers we are protected by God through salvation.

The protective benefits of salvation

I want you to take a moment and look at the protective benefits of salvation that is listed in Psalm 91. These are the benefits that are covered under your salvation policy. I want you to pay special attention to the highlighted portions below.

Psalm 91:1-16 NKJV

*[1] He who dwells in the secret place of the Most High shall **abide under the shadow of the Almighty.** [2] I will say of the LORD, "**He is my refuge and my fortress;** My God, in Him I will trust." [3] Surely **He shall deliver you from the snare** of the fowler and **from the perilous pestilence.** [4] He shall cover you with His feathers, and under His wings you shall take refuge; **His truth shall be your shield and buckler.** [5] **You shall not be afraid** of the terror by night, nor of the arrow that flies by day, [6] Nor of the pestilence that walks in darkness, Nor of the destruction that lays waste at noonday. [7] **A thousand may fall** at your side, and ten thousand at your right hand; **But it shall not come near you.** [8] Only with your eyes shall you look, and see the reward of the wicked. [9] Because you have made the LORD, who is my refuge, Even the Most High, your dwelling place, [10] **No evil shall befall you, Nor shall any plague come near your dwelling;** [11] For **He shall give His angels charge over you,** To keep you in all your ways. [12] In their hands they shall bear you up, Lest you dash your foot against a stone. [13] **You shall tread upon the lion and the cobra, The young lion and the serpent you shall trample underfoot.** [14] Because he has set his love upon Me, therefore **I will deliver him; I will set him on high,** because he has known My name. [15] He shall call upon Me, and **I will answer him; I will be with him in trouble; I will deliver him and honor him.** [16] **With long life I will satisfy him, And show him My salvation.***

When you study Psalm 91 it perfectly lists what God is protecting us from.

Deliverance

We have already seen above that, according to the Greek definition of salvation, salvation is also deliverance. Therefore a person that is saved cannot be demon possessed. They might be demon oppressed, but not demon possessed. There is a difference between possession and oppression. A Christian just can't have a demon in them. Light and darkness do not dwell in the same place.

Deliverance from demonic oppression

Colossians 1:13-14 NKJV
[13] He has delivered us from the power of darkness and conveyed us into the kingdom of the Son of His love, [14] in whom we have redemption through His blood, the forgiveness of sins.

I want you to see in this verse how deliverance from the power of darkness and salvation go hand in hand. Paul says God delivered us from the power of darkness and we have received the forgiveness of sins. The two go hand in hand. When you get saved, Christ comes to dwell in you. When He is in you, no demonic power can dwell in you any longer.

Deliverance from bloodline curses

1 Peter 1:18-19 NIV
[18] For you know that it was not with perishable things such as silver or gold that you were redeemed from the empty way of life handed down to you from your ancestors, [19] but with the precious blood of Christ, a lamb without blemish or defect.

If you are born again, you should not suffer from bloodline curses, unless you ignorantly subject yourself to it. Christ has delivered you from bloodline curses. You should not fear any curses in your family. You may say, "But Pastor, why is it still functioning in me?" It is because you have opened the door for them through fear and ignorance. Cast out any form of bloodline curses by faith with your authority in Christ Jesus.

John 1:12-13 NKJV
[12] But as many as received Him, to them He gave the right to become children of God, to those who believe in His name: [13] who were born, not of blood, nor of the will of the flesh, nor of the will of man, but of God.

Once you are born of God you no longer have the infirmities of your bloodline.

Healing is part of your salvation

Your salvation includes physical, spiritual and emotional healing.

Prayer saves the sick

James 5:15 KJV

[15] And the prayer of faith shall save the sick, and the Lord shall raise him up; and if he has committed sins, they shall be forgiven him.

Did you notice that healing is salvation in this verse? James says the prayer of faith will save the sick.

Salvation is also healing

When Peter healed the crippled man, they were questioned as to how they really healed the man. Then Peter explained to the Jewish council who it was who actually healed the man. In his explanation, Peter referred to the healing of the man as salvation in the name of Jesus.

Acts 4:8-12 NKJV
[8] Then Peter, filled with the Holy Spirit, said to them, "Rulers of the people and elders of Israel: [9] If we this day are judged for a good

deed done to a helpless man, by what means he has been made well, [10] let it be known to you all, and to all the people of Israel, that by the name of Jesus Christ of Nazareth, whom you crucified, whom God raised from the dead, by Him this man stands here before you whole. [11] This is the 'stone which was rejected by you builders, which has become the chief cornerstone.' [12] Nor is there salvation in any other, for there is no other name under heaven given among men by which we must be saved."

Jesus connects healing and salvation

When certain men lowered their friend through the roof on his bed for Jesus to heal him, instead of saying to the man, "You are healed," Jesus said, *"Your sins are forgiven."* Jesus gave him the greater gift. Salvation is the greatest miracle. It includes healing.

Matthew 9:2-6 NKJV
[2] Then behold, they brought to Him a paralytic lying on a bed. When Jesus saw their faith, He said to the paralytic, "Son, be of good cheer; your sins are forgiven you." [3] And at once some of the scribes said within themselves, "This Man blasphemes!" [4] But Jesus, knowing their thoughts, said, "Why do you think evil in your hearts? [5] For which is easier, to say, 'Your sins are forgiven you,' or to say, 'Arise and walk'? [6] But that you may know that the Son of Man has power on earth to forgive sins"- then He said to the paralytic, "Arise, take up your bed, and go to your house."

Jesus instructed many people whom He healed to go and sin no more unless a worst thing should happen to them. Jesus connected sin to sickness. I also want you to know that it does not mean that all people who are sick are living in sin or have committed sin. Sickness just flourishes better in a sinful environment. Sickness is directly from the devil.

How to make the Word work for you

Receive Salvation

Romans 10:9 NKJV
[9] that if you confess with your mouth the Lord Jesus and believe in your heart that God has raised Him from the dead, you will be saved.

In order to activate the benefits of salvation in your life, you have to receive salvation. In order to receive salvation, you have to believe with your heart and confess with your mouth, then you will be saved.

Believe with your heart

You have to believe that first of all Jesus is the son of God and that salvation is in no other name but the name of Jesus **(Acts 4:12).**

Confess with your mouth

Salvation comes through confession. You have to make the confession to salvation with your mouth. There are people who believe in God and Jesus, but they have never made the confession to salvation. They think only their believing makes them a child of God. Some would take their church membership as a ticket to salvation and heaven. Only believing is not enough. James says in **James 2:19** *"You believe that there is one God. You do well. Even the demons believe--and tremble!"* You have to confess your sin and walk in the ways of God.

Speak the Word

Once you are saved you have to believe you have received the benefits of salvation and keep speaking it. Keep declaring what the word of God says about you.

Romans 10:6-9 NKJV

[6] But the righteousness of faith speaks in this way, "Do not say in your heart, 'Who will ascend into heaven?'" (that is, to bring Christ down from above) [7] or, "'Who will descend into the abyss?'" (that is, to bring Christ up from the dead). [8] But what does it say? "The word is near you, in your mouth and in your heart" (that is, the word of faith which we preach): [9] that if you confess with your mouth the Lord Jesus and believe in your heart that God has raised Him from the dead, you will be saved.

The things of the Spirit work with Words of Faith. You have to believe and declare what the Word says.

CHAPTER 3

HEALING

When it comes to the subject of divine healing, it is important to note first of all that God wants you well. God sent His son Jesus to die on the cross and by His stripes we are healed. He made provision for your healing before you could face a single sickness. Think about it for a minute. Many people take flu vaccine before or during the flu season to avoid having to catch the flu. In the same way, God sent Jesus to pay for your healing so you don't have to be sick. God's idea of healing was rather prevention instead of cure. However, He still wants to heal you even if you are already sick.

Biblical facts about healing

- Healing is for our day.
- It is the will of God to heal you.
- Nothing is impossible with God.
- No disease is beyond the miracle-working ability of God.
- God wants you well.

How to receive your healing

In this chapter I want to briefly discuss the above facts about healing. I want you to also examine the Scriptures and be thoroughly convinced, not by an intellectual argument but by the written Word which must become the manifested Word in your life.

Healing is for our day

It will be of no benefit for us to discuss the subject of healing if we are not convinced that divine healing is for our day. Many people, especially Christians, believe that divine healing was for the days of Jesus and the disciples, while medical science is for our day. They think that people who still believe in divine healing are outdated and ignorant of the times we live in. In some cases there are those who once believed in divine healing, but they did not see the results they were hoping for. Some were Pastors who wanted to have a healing ministry and others are ordinary people who desired divine healing. Most of them believe that they had true faith for it to happen, but it did not happen. The truth may sound harsh but they may have missed the mark somewhere, either in faith or in obedience to Scriptural instructions. Kenneth Hagin once said, "Faith will always have Biblical results. If it does not have results, it is not faith." It was a bitter pill for me to swallow at the then infancy stages of my faith, but I have found it to be true.

Divine healing is one of the eternal benefits of the cross. I want us to look at a few scriptures to establish what I have said above.

Laying hands on the sick was part of the great commission and signs of healing follow those who believe in God.

Mark 16:17-18 NKJV
[17] And these signs will follow those who believe: In My name they will cast out demons; they will speak with new tongues; [18] they will take up serpents; and if they drink anything deadly, it will by no

means hurt them; they will lay hands on the sick, and they will recover.

God does not change, He remains the same.

Hebrews 13:8 NKJV
[8] Jesus Christ is the same yesterday, today, and forever.

God has not changed His mind concerning divine healing. He still wants to heal people today.

Divine Healing is one of the signs that confirms the Word a preacher has preached.

Mark 16:20 NKJV
[20] And they went out and preached everywhere, the Lord working with them and confirming the word through the accompanying signs. Amen.

Many people just focus on the scripture that says, *"Many will say in your name we drove out demons and healed the sick and I will say to them I never knew you."* They don't realise that there are others whom God knows. Divine Healing confirms the Word a preacher has preached. A preacher who preaches a Word without signs following is just a historian, no matter how eloquent in speech he might be.

Jesus Himself was accredited by miracles, signs and wonders.

Acts 2:22 NIV
[22] Men of Israel, listen to this: Jesus of Nazareth was a man accredited by God to you by miracles, wonders and signs, which God did among you through him, as you yourselves know.

The world has its way of accrediting its graduates, and God also has His way of accrediting His graduates. A graduate without proper accreditation is an illegal operative.

➤ **It is God's will to heal you**

One day in prayer the Lord told me, "I want you well more than you can ever desire to be well." Those words gave me faith for divine healing for myself and also to pray for others, knowing God will heal them. At one stage when my doctor told me I will have to be on a certain treatment for the rest of my life because of the medical condition I was facing, I had the boldness to believe God for healing, and I received my healing. I have also witnessed the miracle-working power of God through my hands to many who came in faith in search of their healing.

I want you to be convinced that it is God's will to heal you. He sent His son to die for you on the cross and by His stripes you are healed **(1 Peter 2:24, Isaiah 53:5).**

A leper wanted to know if it was the will of Jesus to heal him. Jesus told Him, *"I am willing."*

Luke 5:12-13 NKJV
[12] While Jesus was in one of the towns, a man came along who was covered with leprosy. When he saw Jesus, he fell with his face to the ground and begged him, "Lord, if you are willing, you can make me clean." [13] Jesus reached out his hand and touched the man. "I am willing," he said. "Be clean!" And immediately the leprosy left him.

May you never end your prayer with the doubtful words: "Father, if it is Your will." Exercise your faith. Many people will end their prayer with the words: "Father, if it is Your will, please heal this person." Those words are full of doubt. It is a coward's prayer, because if the person gets healed you will be saying, "I prayed for them and they got healed." If the person dies you will be saying, "It was not the will of God; maybe it was the person's time to die." You are responsible to have faith. Let God do the healing part through your faith. Don't feel like a failure when the person still dies after your prayer. Believe that

God hears you, irrespective of circumstances. Soon your faith will be so high that people will be healed immediately after your prayers.

➤ Nothing is impossible with God

Matthew 4:23 NKJV
[23] And Jesus went about all Galilee, teaching in their synagogues, preaching the gospel of the kingdom, and healing all kinds of sickness and all kinds of disease among the people.

There was no disease in the days of Jesus that was beyond the miracle-working power of God. Jesus healed all diseases. It is still so in our days. We should never forget that we are here because the saints of old made it by the healing power of God. There was no man-made system of health. Their medicine was the word of God. The word of God can still heal us today. Jesus is the same yesterday, today and forevermore.

Most people generally believe that God can heal. Most of their beliefs are based on curable diseases. It is easy to believe that God can heal a curable disease, but how about an incurable disease? Let me ask you this: "How about when you need healing from an incurable disease? Will you still believe that God can heal?" I want you to answer that question with a definite Yes, because God will heal you.

Luke 1:37 NKJV
[37] For with God nothing will be impossible.

Set your mind on the fact that nothing is impossible with God. Refuse to doubt God under any circumstances. Be thoroughly convinced that when you have faith in God there is no such thing as incurable, impossible and unaffordable. Thank God right now and declare healing to every sickness; abundance to every lack; righteousness to every sin; and possibility to every impossibility.

➢ **No condition is beyond the miracle-working power of God**

Jeremiah 32:27
[27] I am the LORD, the God of all mankind. Is anything too hard for me?

There is nothing under the sun for which God will come back to you and report that He could not fix it. Nothing is too hard for God. Nothing is impossible with God. It is good to know that nothing is impossible with God, but it is better to know that you have that God-given divine ability and nothing is impossible for you. Your faith eliminates all impossibilities. Your doubts create impossibilities. So whenever something becomes impossible, I want you to understand that doubt has stepped in. Please note that Jesus says, *"All things are possible to him who believes."* All things means that nothing is excluded.

Your condition

The more you know about your condition, the more challenging it might become for you to believe that God is able to heal you. He can and He will heal you if you can only believe. You have to believe first that God can heal you. Faith is the first action you should take towards God's word. Arm yourself with the Scriptures in the following chapter about healing for any condition.

CHAPTER 4

GOD CAN HEAL ANY CONDITION

In this chapter I want to draw your attention to just a few familiar conditions that God has successfully healed. Let faith come to you for the healing of any condition you may have. If a particular disease you may suffer from is not spelled out here, please don't be a doubting Thomas, but rather catch faith for your healing in the miraculous power of God to heal your condition too.

Epilepsy

Luke 9:38-43 NIV
[38] A man in the crowd called out, "Teacher, I beg you to look at my son, for he is my only child. [39] A spirit seizes him and he suddenly screams; it throws him into convulsions so that he foams at the mouth. It scarcely ever leaves him and is destroying him. [40] I begged your disciples to drive it out, but they could not." [41] "O unbelieving and perverse generation," Jesus replied, "how long shall

I stay with you and put up with you? Bring your son here." [42] Even while the boy was coming, the demon threw him to the ground in a convulsion. But Jesus rebuked the evil spirit, healed the boy and gave him back to his father. [43] And they were all amazed at the greatness of God.

Epileptic attacks are demonic attacks. In the verse above we find that Jesus drove an evil spirit out of the boy who was suffering from epileptic attacks. The good news is that God can heal epileptic attacks.

Sleeplessness (insomnia)

God grants sleep

Psalm 127:2 NKJV
[2] It is vain for you to rise up early, To sit up late, To eat the bread of sorrows; For so He gives His beloved sleep.

Your bed is the place where most mental battles are fought. It is the place where good or bad, fear or faith, sin or righteous thoughts race on the highways of the mind. Anybody can lay their body to rest, but not everybody can lay their mind to rest. The process of falling asleep, as we learn in the above verse, is a gift from God. Many people have to turn to pills to automate the process of sleep, but God grants His beloved sleep. The believer can lie on his bed meditating on the Word and fall asleep peacefully, while others have to battle their way through the night.

As a Christian, God has purposed for you to have a good night's rest. No Christian's sleep should be interrupted by the fear of lack and insufficiency. The Lord is your shepherd and you shall not want. With God your bed can become a place of heavenly dreams, visions and peaceful rest.

Sleep is a gift from God. As a child of God, God wants you to rest well at night. It is the will of God that you enjoy peaceful sleep. Working hard can make you tired and cause you to sleep, but there are many people who work hard, yet find it difficult to sleep. Some sleep just a few hours. They will toss and turn in bed the whole night. God wants to grant you sleep.

God wants you to rest in peace. Most people's idea of resting in peace relates to death. They believe people can rest in peace the day they die. Well, a dead person has no choice. They don't need your instruction to tell them to Rest In Peace. You, as a living person, need to Rest In Peace when you lay your head on the pillow at night.

Fear

Isaiah 41:10
[10] Fear not [there is nothing to fear], for I am with you; do not look around you in terror and be dismayed, for I am your God. I will strengthen and harden you to difficulties, yes, I will help you; yes, I will hold you up and retain you with My [victorious] right hand of rightness and justice.

In most cases fear is baseless and just evil anticipation. When you are with God there is indeed nothing to fear. You can find your refuge in the shelter of God's wings and know that all things will work together for your good. No matter what you are facing, God Himself will lead you safely through it. Just trust Him, He has done it and succeeded with others many times before.

Anxiety

Philippians 4:6-9
[6] Be anxious for nothing, but in everything by prayer and supplication, with thanksgiving, let your requests be made known to God; [7] and the peace of God, which surpasses all understanding, will guard your hearts and minds through Christ Jesus. [8] Finally, brethren, whatever things are true, whatever things are noble, whatever things are just, whatever things are pure, whatever things are lovely, whatever things are of good report, if there is any virtue and if there is anything praiseworthy--meditate on these things. [9]

The things which you learned and received and heard and saw in me, these do, and the God of peace will be with you.

he Apostle Paul gives us the perfect recipe for getting rid of anxiety. He is telling us to pray, give thanks and set our minds on things that are lovely, virtues, of good report and praiseworthy. God is more than able to deal with fear and anxiety.

Raising the dead

Luke 7:12-16
[12] And when He came near the gate of the city, behold, a dead man was being carried out, the only son of his mother; and she was a widow. And a large crowd from the city was with her. [13] When the Lord saw her, He had compassion on her and said to her, "Do not weep." [14] Then He came and touched the open coffin, and those who carried him stood still. And He said, "Young man, I say to you, arise." [15] So he who was dead sat up and began to speak. And He presented him to his mother. [16] Then fear came upon all, and they glorified God, saying, "A great prophet has risen up among us"; and, "God has visited His people."

Death is not final when God is invited into the equation. Lazarus' sisters learned that God can raise the dead **(John 11:21-44).** I have personally witnessed how God revived a lifeless, cold body and gave it life again. No matter what bodily ailment you may suffer from, the Holy Spirit can give life to your mortal (dying) body.

Incurable blood diseases

Mark 5:25-29 NKJV
[25] Now a certain woman had a flow of blood for twelve years, [26] and had suffered many things from many physicians. She had spent all that she had and was no better, but rather grew worse. [27] When she heard about Jesus, she came behind Him in the crowd and touched His garment. [28] For she said, "If only I may touch His clothes, I shall be made well." [29] Immediately the fountain of her

blood was dried up, and she felt in her body that she was healed of the affliction.

The woman with the issue of blood was suffering from an incurable blood disease in her day. When she reached out to Jesus in faith, she received her healing. The doctors of her day could not help her, but God had the cure. I want you to realise that the key to the healing of her incurable blood disease was faith. You've got to take the word of God and rise to a level of faith to receive healing for any infirmity in your blood.

Blindness & deafness

Luke 7:22
*[22] Jesus answered and said to them, "Go and tell John the things you have seen and heard: that the **blind see**, the lame walk, the lepers are cleansed, the **deaf hear,** the dead are raised, the poor have the gospel preached to them."*

Whether a person is born blind and deaf or they became blind or deaf, it does not matter. God can and He will still heal you.

Paralysis

Mark 2:3, 9-12 NKJV
[3] Then they came to Him, bringing a paralytic who was carried by four men. [9] Which is easier, to say to the paralytic, 'Your sins are forgiven you,' or to say, 'Arise, take up your bed and walk'? [10] But that you may know that the Son of Man has power on earth to forgive sins"--He said to the paralytic, [11] "I say to you, arise, take up your bed, and go to your house." [12] Immediately he arose, took up the bed, and went out in the presence of them all, so that all were amazed and glorified God, saying, "We never saw anything like this!"

There is healing in Jesus Christ for any form of paralysis. I have witnessed the healing of the most deformed bodies in healing services with a great man of God, and I have also witnessed God healing paralysis in my own miracle crusades. One case among many that always stands out to me is a man who was wheelchair-bound for twenty-six years. He was not satisfied with the grant money he received from the government every month because he used to make that money in a day. His desperation caused him to have great faith and he came to one of my services and God healed him completely. We can reason and say he was after money or we can recognise that no matter what his motive was, he received what he believed for. If you can just believe, all things are possible.

Cancer

2 Kings 20:6-8
[6] And I will add to your days fifteen years. I will deliver you and this city from the hand of the king of Assyria; and I will defend this city for My own sake, and for the sake of My servant David. [7] Then Isaiah said, "Take a lump of figs." So they took and laid it on the boil, and he recovered. [8] And Hezekiah said to Isaiah, "What is the sign that the LORD will heal me, and that I shall go up to the house of the LORD the third day?"

King Hezekiah had a growth which was initially going to cause his death. When he turned to God and spoke the Word, God healed him and added fifteen more years to his life. No cancerous growth automatically means death if you can believe God and take Him at His word.

God can heal any condition

John 14:13
[13] And I will do whatever you ask in my name, so that the Son may bring glory to the Father.

In this verse Jesus gives us an eternal guarantee to do whatever we ask the Father in His name. The words *will do* in the Greek is the word *poieo* (pronounced poy-eh-o), which simply means to do, to form or to create. Jesus is saying that if you are asking the Father something that does not exist, He will create it for you. So if your sickness is not listed in the scriptures mentioned above, it is covered by this promise of Jesus.

How to receive your healing

Have faith in God

Hebrews 11:6
[6] And without faith it is impossible to please God, because anyone who comes to him must believe that he exists and that he rewards those who earnestly seek him.

Faith is the master key to receive anything from God. Apply your faith to receive from God. Don't have faith in your sickness; have faith in God. Jesus said to many people in the Bible whom He healed, *"Your faith has made you whole."* The woman with the issue of blood touched the hem of His garment, then power left His body and she was healed immediately. Jesus turned and said to her, *"Daughter, your faith has made you whole."* Would you not have thought it was the power that left Jesus' body that healed her? The truth is, many people touched Him and power did not leave Him. The woman's faith caused the healing power of Jesus to flow.

Healing is certain

Mark 16:17-18
[17] And these signs will follow those who believe: In My name they will cast out demons; they will speak with new tongues; [18] they will take up serpents; and if they drink anything deadly, it will by no means hurt them; they will lay hands on the sick, and they will recover.

It is the will of God to heal His children. When you are sick you should not waver between two opinions whether God wants you well or not. It is His will to heal you. In the above verse God guaranteed healing by the laying on of hands. The laying on of hands is one way to receive your healing.

Sickness is demonic oppression

Acts 10:38 NKJV
[38] How God anointed Jesus of Nazareth with the Holy Spirit and with power, who went about doing good and healing all who were oppressed by the devil, for God was with Him.

Sickness is oppression from the devil. Jesus came to heal all that was oppressed by satan. You should never think that God is trying to teach you a lesson or punish your for sin with sickness. Sickness is the work of the devil. You've got to see it that way and get rid of it by faith.

Speak the Word

Hebrews 10:23
[23] Let us hold unswervingly to the hope we profess, for he who promised is faithful.

You've got to confess the word of God. Take to heart the scriptures I am sharing with you about healing and stand upon them. See for yourself in Scripture that it is God's will to heal you. Don't be double-minded about it. Keep declaring, "By His stripes I am healed." Say what the Word says. Speak the Word against all odds. Call the things that are not as though they were. If the circumstances don't change, don't change your confession. Hold fast to it. Be like Shadrack, Meshack and Abednego who said, "We will go down believing." They were prepared to die for their faith, whether God was going to save them or not. Be absolutely certain.

CHAPTER 5

DELIVERANCE

Deliverance is the act of setting someone free from bondage. In a scriptural context we refer to the act of setting someone free from demon possession or demonic oppression. Later on I will explain the vast difference between demonic oppression and demon possession. Deliverance is a very controversial subject in the church today.

A few years ago it seemed that if you were a deliverance preacher in Africa, you could easily draw people's attention. Then it became famous to be a strange preacher who used funny things with weird demonstrations. Later on, inexperienced youngsters thought if they could be a Prophet their church will grow fast. Some became sons of prophets just to chase the prophetic gifting, without honouring the Prophet. They followed Prophets because they wanted an impartation of their gifting and anointing. What they did not know is that most prophets got their gifting authentically from God and by honouring their spiritual fathers. There will always be people who want to take shortcuts in ministry, with weird demonstrations and showmanship, to draw a crowd quickly. It is not a new thing.

When it comes to the subject of deliverance it is needful for us to look at it from a scriptural point of view. Jesus is our role model and we will start by looking at how He did it.

Jesus cast out demons with a word

Matthew 8:16 NKJV
[16] When evening had come, they brought to Him many who were demon-possessed. And He cast out the spirits with a word, and healed all who were sick.

Matthew 8:28-32 NKJV
[28] When He had come to the other side, to the country of the Gergesenes, there met Him two demon-possessed men, coming out of the tombs, exceedingly fierce, so that no one could pass that way. [29] And suddenly they cried out, saying, "What have we to do with You, Jesus, You Son of God? Have You come here to torment us before the time?" [30] Now a good way off from them there was a herd of many swine feeding. [31] So the demons begged Him, saying, "If You cast us out, permit us to go away into the herd of swine." [32] And He said to them, "Go." So when they had come out, they went into the herd of swine. And suddenly the whole herd of swine ran violently down the steep place into the sea, and perished in the water.

In the days of Jesus on the earth He cast out demons with a word of authority. He did not allow demons to disrupt His services. He displayed the power of God and not the strength and disorder of demonic spirits.

Strange deliverance practices

Vomiting

There are people who believe they should vomit when they are delivered from demonic possession. During the time of brother Kenneth Hagin in the 1980's there were people who would bring buckets into the church and encourage people to vomit into them during times of deliverance. Brother Hagin publicly spoke up against it and declared such practices to be unscriptural.

I once had a lady for counselling who was unhappily married and she had seen disasters and disappointments for most of her years after her marriage. She told me her problems started after her mother-in-law gave her bread with polony on it. I could see that she was expecting to vomit when I pray for her. I first built her up with the scriptures and then I asked her, "Have you been to the toilet since you have eaten the bread and polony?" She frowned and said, "Yes, of cause Pastor." I said, "That's good. I just wanted to make sure if the bread with the polony is out of your stomach. I am sure it is out by now because you ate it almost twenty years ago, but now I am going to drive it out of your spirit and out of your mind." I prayed for her and commanded the demon to leave. She was freed and she became prosperous like never before.

Salvatio includes deliverance

It is important to understand that salvation includes deliverance. You are saved from the power of darkness and translated into the kingdom of light.

Colossians 1:13 NKJV
For he has rescued us from the dominion of darkness and brought us into the kingdom of the Son he loves.

In the Greek the word for salvation is *soteria* which means deliverance from sin, deliverance from the enemy (the devil), salvation and redemption.

Demon possession vs demon oppression

I want you to understand that there is a difference between demonic possession and demonic oppression.

Acts 10:38 NKJV

[38] How God anointed Jesus of Nazareth with the Holy Spirit and with power, who went about doing good and healing all who were oppressed by the devil, for God was with Him.

Demonic oppression

In Jesus' ministry throughout the New Testament we see that He delivered people from sicknesses that were caused by both demonic oppression and possession. Demonic oppression is when a demon oppresses the person. A demon can oppress a Christian who is spiritually ignorant or weak. Such oppression can manifest in the form of sickness, lack, and emotional problems. The devil might not possess the Christian but it is possible for him to oppress a Christian.

With demonic oppression the person is still in control. This is the realm where people play with sin. It is people who can control their addictions. You find a person can be on drugs but they can cleverly control their usage. Or the person consumes alcohol but they only drink on weekends and not during workdays. They are still in control of their craving for alcohol. They can't leave alcohol completely, but they can stay away from it for a while. That can be demonic oppression.

Another term that I also want to add here is "demonic influence." Demonic influence can be when a person is weak in faith and they fall for what the devil is whispering to them. One day the Apostle Peter was rebuking Jesus and Jesus identified the influence behind Peter's words as satan.

Matthew 16:21-23

From that time Jesus began to show to His disciples that He must go to Jerusalem, and suffer many things from the elders and chief priests and scribes, and be killed, and be raised the third day. [22] Then Peter took Him aside and began to rebuke Him, saying, "Far be it from You, Lord; this shall not happen to You!" [23] But He turned and said to Peter, "Get behind Me, Satan! You are an offense to Me, for you are not mindful of the things of God, but the things of men."

Jesus identified the words Peter had spoken as the words of satan. The devil will always try to whisper doubt, fear and unbelief in your ears. Don't allow him to draw you into defeat. Identify his works and rebuke him. It is also important to note that Jesus did not refer to Peter as satan, but to the words he was speaking. Jesus identified those words to have been influenced by satan.

Demon possession

With demonic possession the person has lost his will-power. This is where demons take charge of the person. They speak through them with different voices. A demon might also speak through a person who is oppressed, yet the person can control it. But with possession the person is not in charge and they cannot control it. It is at this stage where a person becomes addicted to for example alcohol, drugs, gambling, smoking, etc. Such a person will take their last money and spend it on their addiction without thinking twice.

You'll find a person might end up stealing or selling possessions of their loved ones. Many times those people genuinely want to be free, but they have lost their will-power. It is at this stage that you find the enemy encouraging many of them to commit suicide or to just completely let go of their life. The good news is that it is never too late for such people. There is hope, and God can deliver them. Such a person needs help and support. Through prayer that demon can be cast out immediately and the person can be free, or the person must be removed from their immediate surroundings and be built up with the Word. This is also where Christian-based rehabilitation centres come in handy.

Not all people who are demon possessed are necessarily addicts. Some are just tormented by evil spirits. They can also be delivered through the casting out of devils.

Can a Christian be demon possessed?

To be demon possessed means to be entirely under the control of demons. It means the person has no control over their passions and their actions. The person is possessed by the devil. A Christian cannot be demon possessed. The minute the person is demon possessed they are no longer a Christian. God is light and in Him there is no darkness. God is that light that shines into darkness, and darkness cannot stand it. Darkness flees at the speed of light when light enters.

A Christian might be demon oppressed. When a Christian is sick or defeated they might be demon oppressed, but never possessed. There are Christians who also suffer depression, fear, anxiety, sickness and sleeplessness. They are not possessed by demons; they are oppressed by demons. They can have their deliverance the minute they use their authority in Christ Jesus and cast those devils off.

Different forms of demonic oppression and possession

Fear (Depression, anxiety, sleeplessness)

Fear is a demonic spirit and it is not from God. It is from satan. God will never use fear or fearful experiences to punish His children. God used His love through the death and resurrection of Jesus Christ to redeem us. As far as He is concerned we are forgiven and provided for if we can only believe and receive it. The enemy will use the spirit of fear to intimidate and destroy you, but fear is never from God.

2 Timothy 1:7 NKJV
[7] For God has not given us a spirit of fear, but of power and of love and of a sound mind.

Addiction

An addiction of any kind, whether it be drugs, sex, alcohol, food or gambling, can either be demon possession or oppression. When a person is still in control of the addiction it might just be demonic oppression. But when the person is driven by the addiction, then they might be demon possessed.

Muteness

They brought a mute person to Jesus and after Jesus drove out the demon the person was healed. Throughout the ministry of Jesus we see various cases where sicknesses were caused by demonic spirits.

Matthew 9:32-33 NKJV
[32] As they went out, behold, they brought to Him a man, mute and demon-possessed. [33] And when the demon was cast out, the mute spoke. And the multitudes marvelled, saying, "It was never seen like this in Israel!"

Blindness and deafness can also be the result of demonic possession

Matthew 12:22-23 NKJV
[22] Then one was brought to Him who was demon-possessed, blind and mute; and He healed him, so that the blind and mute man both spoke and saw. [23] And all the multitudes were amazed and said, "Could this be the Son of David?"

Epilepsy

Matthew 17:14-15, 18 NKJV
[14] And when they had come to the multitude, a man came to Him, kneeling down to Him and saying, [15] "Lord, have mercy on my son, for he is an epileptic and suffers severely; for he often falls into the fire and often into the water." [18] And Jesus rebuked the demon, and it came out of him; and the child was cured from that very hour.

How to be free from demonic activity

A person that is oppressed or possessed by demonic spirits can definitely be freed. I want to give you a few short steps to freedom from demonic possession or oppression.

➢ You must want to be free

You must want to be free from demonic activity. There are people who enjoy the attention they get under the influence of demonic spirits. They don't really desire freedom. They would just like to tell others of their weird experiences. The first requirement for your freedom is the desire to be free. One cannot help people who do not want to help themselves.

➢ Surrender your life totally

Ephesians 4:27 NKJV
[27] nor give place to the devil.

Many people have violent manifestations when the power of God comes upon them. They scream a violent scream and others start manifesting profusely. Many of them really want to be free, but they are still holding on to certain things. Most of the time they are holding on to sinful practices. Other times they are walking with unforgiveness or stubbornness. They might not have forgiven their parents or someone who has hurt them. Some of them are really sincere. They have a true desire for God but they are bitter in soul. They have not let go of their past hurts totally.

When the Holy Spirit comes upon them it's really a fight. They have a violent manifestation when the power comes upon them. There are also others who might still secretly mess around with sin and they ride the roller coaster of asking forgiveness and truly repenting when they come to church, but they go back and throw themselves back into sinful living when they are away from church.

The key to deliverance is to surrender totally to God. You must give no place to the devil. You must say what Jesus said in **John 14:30 AMP** *"I will not talk with you much more, for the prince (evil genius, ruler) of the world is coming. And he has no claim on Me. [He has nothing in common with Me; there is nothing in Me that belongs to him, and he has no power over Me.]"*

➢ Resist the devil and he will flee

James 4:7 NKJV
[7] Therefore submit to God. Resist the devil and he will flee from you.

When you come for deliverance, you have a major part to play. You will have to resist the devil in order to fully lay hold of your freedom. You have to take charge and command the enemy to leave your life. You can't just sit there thinking everything is going to go away magically.

➢ Don't nurture demonic activity

You might find it surprising, but there are people who like to be in another state of mind. They like to slip into a split personality as a form of escape from the real world. So for such people it becomes difficult to really get wilfully free from demonic activity. They enjoy the temporary escape, but they don't like the side effects. As ministers of the Spirit we can command those demons to flee, whether the person participates or not, and they will definitely flee. But to keep them out is the key. That person will have to resist the devil when he tries to come back.

➢ Receive your deliverance by faith

When you are delivered from demonic activity, you also have to receive your deliverance by faith. Don't wait for a spectacular display or manifestation. Remember Naaman was offended because of the way the Prophet Elijah delivered him from leprosy. He had his own preconceived idea of how the Prophet should have done it.

2 Kings 5:11
But Naaman was angry and went away and said, Behold, I thought he would surely come out to me and stand and call on the name of the Lord his God, and wave his hand over the place and heal the leper.

Lay hold of your deliverance by faith. Don't let your own preconceived ideas be a hindrance to your healing. Don't prolong your suffering like Naaman did.

➢ Keep the devil out

Jesus told many people to go and sin no more after He had set them free. In the same way it is important for a person who has been delivered from demonic activity to now occupy their spirit with the Spirit of God. There are people who go to church just to get their deliverance, their healing or their blessing. Many of them have turned out worse afterwards because of what is explained in the Bible.

Matthew 12:43-45
When an unclean spirit goes out of a man, he goes through dry places, seeking rest, and finds none. [44] Then he says, "I will return to my house from which I came." And when he comes, he finds it empty, swept, and put in order. [45] Then he goes and takes with him seven other spirits more wicked than himself, and they enter and dwell there; and the last state of that man is worse than the first. So shall it also be with this wicked generation.

You got to keep the devil out and let Christ dwell in your heart richly.

➢ Believe you are free indeed

John 8:36 NKJV
[36] Therefore if the Son makes you free, you shall be free indeed.

Once you have been delivered from demon possession you have to believe that you are free. There is no need to wonder if you are free. Don't let the enemy tell you lies; you are free indeed. Keep believing and declaring it.

Are demons stronger than Christians?

No, not at all.

1 John 4:4 NKJV
[4] You are of God, little children, and have overcome them, because He who is in you is greater than he who is in the world.

Does a Christian have more authority than demons?

Yes indeed. Christians have a higher authority than the devil. Only sinners are lower in authority than demons. Therefore a sinner needs to get saved first to fight the work of the devil successfully in his life. As a Christian, you are far above all devils and demons. They are not higher than you. You can cast them down. Read what the Apostle Paul writes to understand your position in the realm of the Spirit.

Ephesians 1:15-23 NKJV
[15] Therefore I also, after I heard of your faith in the Lord Jesus and your love for all the saints, [16] do not cease to give thanks for you, making mention of you in my prayers: [17] that the God of our Lord Jesus Christ, the Father of glory, may give to you the spirit of wisdom and revelation in the knowledge of Him, [18] the eyes of your understanding being enlightened; that you may know what is the hope of His calling, what are the riches of the glory of His inheritance in the saints, [19] and what is the exceeding greatness of His power toward us who believe, according to the working of His mighty power [20] which He worked in Christ when He raised Him from the dead and seated Him at His right hand in the heavenly places, [21] far above all principality and power and might and dominion, and every name that is named, not only in this age but also in that which

is to come. [22] And He put all things under His feet, and gave Him to be head over all things to the church, [23] which is His body, the fullness of Him who fills all in all.

How do I cast out demons?

You have to have faith and take authority, as you have seen in the Scriptures that greater is He that is in you than he that is in the world **(1 John 4:4).** You need to know that you have a higher spiritual rank than any demon, according to **Ephesians 1:15-23.** You don't have to play with demons and have conversations with them. You can just command them to leave a person and they will go.

Is it scriptural to have a whole service just casting out demons?

Demons also manifested while Jesus was teaching and I want you to see how He responded. Jesus would drive out a demon by just saying, "Go," and then He would continue with His sermon. Look at the following verse:

Matthew 8:16 NKJV
[16] When evening had come, they brought to Him many who were demon-possessed. And He cast out the spirits with a word, and healed all who were sick.

Did you notice that Jesus drove out demons with just a word? He did not dedicate much time to the act of deliverance. Remember when Jesus drove out the demons from the man into the pigs? He just told them in one word to "Go," and they went. He did not waste much time with them.

Matthew 8:31-32 NKJV
[31] So the demons begged Him, saying, "If You cast us out, permit us to go away into the herd of swine." [32] And He said to them, "Go." So when they had come out, they went into the herd of swine.

And suddenly the whole herd of swine ran violently down the steep place into the sea, and perished in the water.

One word was enough for Jesus to drive out demons. You have the same authority. Don't waste time with demons. Just command them to go!

Is it scriptural to speak to demons?

In most cases Jesus did not allow demons to speak while He was driving them out. There was a time however when He asked the demon in the person, "How many are you?" and the demon said "Legion" and Jesus drove them all out. He did not necessarily have a whole conversation with the demons to tell Him how they operate and how they destroy people's lives.

Mark 1:34 NKJV
[34] Then He healed many who were sick with various diseases, and cast out many demons; and He did not allow the demons to speak, because they knew Him.

Satan is a liar from the beginning. So Jesus did not allow demons to speak.

Luke 4:41 NKJV
[41] And demons also came out of many, crying out and saying, "You are the Christ, the Son of God!" And He, rebuking them, did not allow them to speak, for they knew that He was the Christ.

Firstly Jesus did not allow demons to speak and secondly He did not allow them to accredit Him. Jesus did not need demons to tell people that He was the son of God. He did not need any accreditation from satan. No Man of God should yearn for accreditation from the devil. God accredits us. We are not moved by demons who say we are true servants of God. They can turn around tomorrow and tell the same people the direct opposite and destroy their trust in God, or in us as His servants.

Can a demon go from one person in a service to another?

There is no scriptural reference whereby a demon has gone out of one person into another. However, Jesus did drive demons out of one person and allowed them to go into the pigs.

I know that there are services where people are told they should be careful because the demons that have been driven out can go into them. When demons are driven out they are abandoned to waterless places, unless the person in authority tells them to go and occupy another vessel.

If you are in a service where the presence of God is, and demons are driven out, you are under the protection of God. If you are a born again Christian a demon can also not enter you because Christ is already living in you. Light and darkness cannot share the same room. So you don't have to fear that demons will flee into you. You are well protected.

John 1:5 AMP
[5] And the Light shines on in the darkness, for the darkness has never overpowered it [put it out or absorbed it or appropriated it, and is unreceptive to it].

Is it scripturally correct to study the kingdom of darkness?

There are people who study the kingdom of darkness with the idea of having an understanding of how the devil works so they can be aware of his tactics. The truth is we have enough scriptural references that tell us that we are on the winning side. The Greater One lives in us. Greater is He that is in us than he that is in the world. Our fight is indeed against powers and principalities, but we are seated far above all powers and principalities. It will be more beneficial and effective for you to study your authority in Christ. The devil will not pay you any reward for studying his kingdom, but he will try to intimidate you. Rather study the kingdom of light and you will have greater power and authority over the devil

CHAPTER 6

RIGHTEOUSNESS

1 Peter 3:12
[12] For the eyes of the LORD are on the righteous, And His ears are open to their prayers; But the face of the LORD is against those who do evil.

God keeps watch over those who walk in righteousness before Him. He hears their prayers.

What does it mean to be righteous?

- Righteousness is God's requirement for His followers.
- Righteousness is the ability to be right and right only.
- It means to be in right standing with God.

So, in our opening verse we learn that a person who is right and right only is in right standing with God and God will watch over them and answer their prayers.

Pastor Gerald Hugo

Who is righteous?

Do you think there is a human person who can be right and right only, which means the person never commits a single wrong? We learn in **Romans 3:10-12** *As it is written: "There is none righteous, no, not one; There is none who understands; There is none who seeks after God. They have all turned aside; They have together become unprofitable; There is none who does good, no, not one."*

So righteousness, according to human standards, disqualifies all mankind from having a relationship with God or receiving anything from Him.

Two kinds of righteousness

In the Scriptures we find two kinds of righteousness:

- There is a righteousness that is the result of good works, which is called the righteousness of the law.
- And there is a righteousness which is the result of your faith in God.

The righteousness of the law

The righteousness of the law simply means if you obey the Ten Commandments and all the other laws in the books of the law, you are righteous. The Apostle Paul was grieved when he saw that the Israelites were still trying to be righteous by following the law.

Romans 10:1-3
[1] Brethren, my heart's desire and prayer to God for Israel is that they may be saved. [2] For I bear them witness that they have a zeal for God, but not according to knowledge. [3] For they, being ignorant of God's righteousness, and seeking to establish their own righteousness, have not submitted to the righteousness of God.

The righteousness of the law states that one has to obey the Ten Commandments in order to be counted righteous. The Apostle Paul

50

was praying for the children of Israel because they tried to pursue God through the Law. They did not recognise that Jesus was the way to God. God has already found the Law to be insufficient for Righteousness, therefore He sent Jesus. No man was made perfect by the Law. The law was a good school master to lead us to Christ.

Most people want to live holy and obey God. So their starting point for Holiness is the law. They would go to the Ten Commandments and try to live holy. That is a good place to start, but it is not the ultimate way, as you will see. The fulfilment of the law is your own efforts to try and be righteous.

Israel was trying to reach God through their own efforts. They were trying to be righteous so God could accept them. But God gave us Jesus that we might accept His righteousness. Many times people want to clean themselves before they come to God. They want to make themselves righteous. That's what the Israelites were trying to do. The problem with trying to reach God with your own righteousness is that you can easily turn into a critic and become self-righteous by comparing yourself to others.

Some people would say, "I want to serve God, but the day I get saved I am not going to be like that sister who is still doing this or that. I am not going to be like that brother." They feel a sense of superiority and self-righteousness. They want to save themselves first and say to God, "Here I am, holy and perfect."

Jesus told the story of the tax collector and the Pharisee who went up to the temple to pray. The Pharisee was self-righteous and he boasted in what he did right. The tax collector just begged for mercy. And Jesus said the prayer of the tax collector was accepted. The scribes and Pharisees also wanted to know why Jesus was always among the sinners and not among those who are righteous. Jesus told them it is the sick who need a doctor and not those who are healed. We cannot save ourselves. We cannot cleanse ourselves. Our good works are like filthy rags in the sight of God.

Isaiah 64:6

[6] But we are all like an unclean thing, And all our righteousnesses are like filthy rags; We all fade as a leaf, And our iniquities, like the wind, have taken us away.

In Hebrew the words "filthy rags" refer to the same word that was used in Leviticus for the menstrual cloth, which means our own works of righteousness is like the old menstrual cloth. It is stained with human blood and therefore still dirty. Our own blood cannot save us. It makes us dirty. The blood of Jesus is the only blood in which we can dip our garments that can make our garments white as snow.

Revelation 7:13-14

[13] Then one of the elders answered, saying to me, "Who are these arrayed in white robes, and where did they come from?" [14] And I said to him, "Sir, you know." So he said to me, "These are the ones who come out of the great tribulation, and washed their robes and made them white in the blood of the Lamb."

Hallelujah. This is so glorious. We can take our dirty white garments and wash them in the red blood of Jesus and they become pure white. That is what the blood of Jesus has done for our sin.

The law brought sin-consciousness and not righteousness

Romans 7:7-10

[7] What shall we say then? Is the law sin? Certainly not! On the contrary, I would not have known sin except through the law. For I would not have known covetousness unless the law had said, "You shall not covet." [8] But sin, taking opportunity by the commandment, produced in me all manner of evil desire. For apart from the law sin was dead. [9] I was alive once without the law, but when the commandment came, sin revived and I died. [10] And the commandment, which was to bring life, I found to bring death.

The Apostle Paul states here that something is right until a law is made against it. He says that the law brought a sin-consciousness. As a result, the law caused people to feel guilty all the time. Instead of causing righteousness, the law brought guilt. When man became guilty, he was now subject to punishment. The judgement of the law was death. So Paul is saying the law, which was supposed to bring life, brought death.

One failure breaks the whole law

James 2:10-11
[10] For whoever shall keep the whole law, and yet stumble in one point, he is guilty of all. [11] For He who said, "Do not commit adultery," also said, "Do not murder." Now if you do not commit adultery, but you do murder, you have become a transgressor of the law.

The problem with the law was that one mistake can nullify all your efforts of holiness. If you make just one mistake, you have broken the whole law. So God seeks to make provision for us.

Galatians 3:21
[21] Is the law then against the promises of God? Certainly not! For if there had been a law given which could have given life, truly righteousness would have been by the law.

The major failures of the law

The three major areas where the law failed were:

1. It made no person righteous, as I have explained above.
2. The law brought sin-consciousness and not righteousness.
3. One mistake makes a person a transgressor of the entire law.

We are therefore all in desperate need of the righteousness of God which is in Christ Jesus.

The righteousness of God

Through the death and resurrection of Jesus Christ we were placed under the grace of God that gave us righteousness by faith. We are no longer under the righteousness of the law. We are now under the righteousness of God.

Romans 10:4-5
[4] For Christ is the end of the law for righteousness to everyone who believes. [5] For Moses writes about the righteousness which is of the law, "The man who does those things shall live by them."

Christ brought an end to the righteousness that was brought by the law. The righteousness of the law was imperfect. It could not clear the conscience of the worshipper who drew near to God, but it was rather a reminder of sin **(Hebrews 10:2-4).**

The new law

When we say that Christ is the end of the law and we are no longer under Law but under Grace, a person might say, "You see, even God realised it is hard not to commit adultery and fornication. He understands; we are under Grace." That is why you find people who comfortably continue in their sin, thinking everybody is going to heaven because God is a loving father and we are all under Grace. They are sincerely mistaken. You need to complete your study in full. You can't just draw a conclusion halfway into the study of Grace. To say we are no longer under the Law is just half the story. What are we under right now? We need to complete the story. Here it is in the following verses:

Romans 13:9-10
[9] For the commandments, "You shall not commit adultery, You shall not murder, You shall not steal, You shall not bear false witness, You shall not covet," and if there is any other commandment, are all summed up in this saying, namely, "You shall

love your neighbor as yourself." [10] Love does no harm to a neighbor; therefore love is the fulfillment of the law.

The love of God has become the new law. Instead of telling us a lot of *don'ts*, God has given us one *do* that will fulfil all the don'ts. Love covers the entire law. You can actually take the new law of love and read the Ten Commandments and see if, when you love, you will really break the Ten Commandments. You will notice that love fulfils the whole Law effortlessly.

How to receive the righteousness of God

- Believe that God made you righteous.
- Receive the righteousness of God as a gift.
- Receive righteousness by faith.

Believe that you were made righteous

2 Corinthians 5:21 KJV
[21] For he hath made him to be sin for us, who knew no sin; that we might be made the righteousness of God in him.

We are the righteousness of God in Christ. Christ was made sin that we might be made the righteousness of God. Some translations might say that we might become the righteousness of God. That is the wrong word. The word is that we might be made the righteousness of God as it is displayed in the King James Version above. The word *become* suggests a process. It means you are metamorphosing from a sinner to a saint, which means it takes time. But that is not what Paul meant. He meant when Jesus was made sin, at that very moment we were made the righteousness of God. Which means it is not a process. The Greek word for *made* is *ginomai*. It means to cause to be.

As a Christian, you are not striving toward righteousness. Righteousness is a state of being. You are righteous. Christ has caused you to be righteous. You are in a state of righteousness. You are not striving toward righteousness. Many people, after having been saved for five years, say God is still dealing with them to perfect them. They say so because they observe their shortcomings. What they don't know is that at the moment they believed, they were made righteous; they are not striving toward righteousness. They will see a change immediately.

When you know you are righteous before God, not because of your own goodness but because of the blood of Jesus, it gives you confidence toward God and you can ask anything without a doubt and receive it.

Receive the gift of righteousness

Romans 5:17
[17] For if by the one man's offense death reigned through the one, much more those who receive abundance of grace and of the gift of righteousness will reign in life through the One, Jesus Christ.

Righteousness is God's gift unto us. It is not a reward for good behaviour; it is a gift of God's love. God loved us and He gave us a gift that will make us receive all that we need. Receive the gift of righteousness God has already given you. Just receive it.

Receive righteousness by faith

We know that righteousness is God's gift to us. We know that God made us righteous by the death of Jesus Christ. So how do we walk in it? We need to walk in it by faith. There is no tangible token that will prove we are righteous. You need to believe that God has made you righteous.

Romans 3:22
[22] even the righteousness of God, through faith in Jesus Christ, to all and on all who believe. For there is no difference.

Romans 1:16-17
[16] For I am not ashamed of the gospel of Christ, for it is the power of God to salvation for everyone who believes, for the Jew first and also for the Greek. [17] For in it the righteousness of God is revealed from faith to faith; as it is written, "The just shall live by faith."

When you are commanding sickness out of your life, driving out devils, or asking anything from God, don't let the devil condemn you over your past mistakes. Be bold and full of Faith. Receive righteousness by Faith.

I want you to read the following two verses meditatively and look upon some benefits of righteousness.

Romans 8:1 NKJV
[1] There is therefore now no condemnation to those who are in Christ Jesus, who do not walk according to the flesh, but according to the Spirit.

Hebrews 4:16 NKJV
[16] Let us therefore come boldly to the throne of grace, that we may obtain mercy and find grace to help in time of need.

God has made you right and right only

Galatians 2:16
[16] knowing that a man is not justified by the works of the law but by faith in Jesus Christ, even we have believed in Christ Jesus, that we might be justified by faith in Christ and not by the works of the law; for by the works of the law no flesh shall be justified.

No person is justified by the works of the law, therefore we need the righteousness of God. Right living for you should be the result of righteousness and not the source of righteousness. Which means you don't feel righteous because you did right; you feel righteous because God made you righteous and therefore you choose to do right. Jesus should be the source of your righteousness and not your own works.

Righteousness refers to the Rightness of God; the very nature of God to be right. God cannot be wrong. God Himself is the standard for righteousness. God has the ability to be right and right only which no one else ever had. God gave it to us as a gift. He gave us the ability to stand in His presence without a sense of guilt or condemnation.

You can stand before God with this gift of righteousness and come boldly before Him and receive desired answers to all your requests. Hallelujah!

The benefits of the righteousness of God

- God's ear is attentive to the Prayer of the Righteous.
- The prayer of a righteous man avails much.
- Wealth and riches are in the house of the righteous.
- All things are added to the righteous.
- It gives you boldness to drive out demons.
- You have authority over the devil.

CHAPTER 7

UNDERSTANDING LAW AND GRACE

It is important to understand that where rules do not govern an atmosphere, abuse is at the order of the day. In every organisation there have to be rules that prescribe expectations and responsibilities and direct conduct. Where there are no rules you will be abused, or you will abuse others, and you will abuse the organisation. Rules and regulations serve as a form of protection for the bodies and entities involved. Lawlessness promotes abuse. A person who hates rules hates discipline. In the Bible these regulations were referred to as The Law.

In this chapter I want to share with you some understanding regarding Law and Grace. It is therefore needful for us to start at the very beginning. I will draw a short timeline to show how it all started and where we are now.

The timeline

In the beginning God created the heavens and the earth. God also created the first two human beings ever to set foot on the earth. Adam and Eve fell into sin and they were banished out of the Garden of Eden. Their son Cain committed the first murder, by murdering his brother Able. As time went by and men started filling the earth, man became extremely evil.

Noah

God found that man, whom He had created, had become evil. He said in Genesis, *"Their waking thoughts were evil."* They were constantly looking for ways and means to commit sin. God decided to bring an end to the world and to start all over again with one man. God found Noah to be that faithful man. God then destroyed the earth with water through a flood and saved Noah and his family in an ark.

Abraham

After Noah's death there was one language on the earth and the people decided to build a tower to make a name for themselves. So God came down and confused their language, and they were scattered all over the earth.

God found Him another man, called Abraham, and He made Abraham a promise. It was an unconditional promise. This was to be the last man God was now starting over with. The promise God made to Abraham had no conditions attached to it. God made an eternal covenant with Abraham and told him that his people will be slaves in a foreign land for four hundred years, but they will eventually be free.

God also gave Abraham a promise that He will make him into a great nation. So God was now building a new nation again.

Genesis 15:13 NIV
[13] Then the Lord said to him, "Know for certain that for four hundred years your descendants will be strangers in a country not their own and that they will be enslaved and mistreated there."

Exodus 12:40-41 NIV
[40] Now the length of time the Israelite people lived in Egypt was 430 years. [41] At the end of the 430 years, to the very day, all the Lord's divisions left Egypt.

Isaac

Isaac was Abraham's son of promise. The blessing that God had placed upon Abraham was now placed on Isaac, because the blessing was a generational blessing. Isaac had two sons called Jacob and Esau, and Isaac transferred the blessing onto his son Jacob.

Jacob
Esau sold his blessing to his brother Esau for lentil soup, but when his father wanted to bless him Esau did not tell his father that he had sold his first-born right. He was unfair, but his mother saw everything and she fixed it. Jacob got the blessing and that same night he had to flee for his life from his father's house with nothing in his hand, because his brother wanted to kill him. The blessing was rightfully his, because his brother sold it to him in a legal transaction.

He worked for his uncle and the blessing began to work in his life. He finally decided to go back to his father's house. When he went back he doubted whether his brother had forgiven him. That night he had an all-night prayer and the angel of the Lord came to him. He laid hold of the angel and told the angel, *"I will not leave you until you bless me."* He was already a blessed man. He had many material possessions, but this time he wanted spiritual blessings. He did not want a blessing from his natural father; he wanted a blessing from God. The angel touched his hip and told him, *"From now on your name shall be called Israel."*

Jacob had twelve sons and his sons became the children of Israel. They were divided into twelve tribes and those twelve tribes are together called the children of Israel. That is where the famous reference to the people of God as *Israel* comes from. It was Jacob who was one single man but God made a nation out of him.

This was the same promise that was on his forefather Abraham that was now at work in him. He had twelve sons and one of his sons was called Joseph. Joseph was hated by his brothers because of his dreams, so they sold him as a slave.

Joseph

Joseph was sold as a slave and went through the pit to the palace, then to the prison and back to the palace again. As he worked for Pharaoh he became the governor of Egypt and that is how he brought his whole family to Egypt. All Joseph's brothers, the sons of Jacob, went to live in Egypt with Joseph their brother where he was the governor. They lived a good life, working for Pharaoh.

A Pharaoh that knew not Joseph

There arose a Pharaoh that knew not Joseph and he felt threatened by the children of Israel who increased in the land, thus he made them slaves. He oppressed them and what God had told Abraham that your descendants will be slaves was now happening to them. Joseph reminded the children of Israel about the promise of God that they will be delivered. He told them that the day God delivers them they should not leave his bones in a grave in Egypt, but they should take his bones with them.

Exodus 1:8-10
[8] Now there arose a new king over Egypt, who did not know Joseph.[9] And he said to his people, "Look, the people of the children of Israel are more and mightier than we; [10] come, let us deal shrewdly with them, lest they multiply, and it happen, in the

event of war, that they also join our enemies and fight against us, and so go up out of the land."

Moses

God found a man called Moses, born to one of the Israelite women, and God called and prepared him to lead the Israelites out of Egypt. He had to walk with God and fight against Pharaoh. God brought plagues on Egypt and showed them wonders until Pharaoh gave in and agreed to let them go. God also dealt with their enemy in the Red Sea, once and for all. It was when they found themselves in the desert that God gave them rules and regulations of how they should behave themselves.

The Law

God gave the Law to Moses as rules and regulations that will govern them until they enter the Promised Land. God's idea for them was not that they should live under the law all their lives, but that they should live under the blessing of Abraham. The purpose of the law was to serve unto them as a school master that they would grow closer to God and live a godly life.

The Ten Commandments

When the Israelites were in bondage in Egypt they were under the rule of Pharaoh. They all had their individual households. In their households they each had their own rules that governed their families. As they were travelling through the desert on their way to the Promised Land they had become one big community in transit with all their possessions in their hands. They became envious toward what they saw their neighbours had. They stole among one another because of greed. They saw their neighbours' wives and were in each other's space all day long. They also came from Egypt where Pharaoh worshipped foreign God's as they were working there. So all of these challenges arose in the desert.

Now it was needful for them to have a set of rules and principles by which they should conduct themselves. It was at this stage that God called Moses up to Mount Sinai and gave him ten commandments. The Ten Commandments addressed the problems they were facing and gave them direction of how they should conduct themselves. These were the Ten Commandments:

Exodus 20:3-17
[3] You shall have no other gods before me.
[4] You shall not make for yourself an idol in the form of anything in heaven above or on the earth beneath or in the waters below.
[5] You shall not bow down to them or worship them; for I, the LORD your God, am a jealous God, punishing the children for the sin of the fathers to the third and fourth generation of those who hate me, [6] but showing love to a thousand {generations} of those who love me and keep my commandments.
[7] You shall not misuse the name of the LORD your God, for the LORD will not hold anyone guiltless who misuses his name.
[8] Remember the Sabbath day by keeping it holy. [9] Six days you shall labor and do all your work, [10] but the seventh day is a Sabbath to the LORD your God. On it you shall not do any work, neither you, nor your son or daughter, nor your manservant or maidservant, nor your animals, nor the alien within your gates. [11] For in six days the LORD made the heavens and the earth, the sea, and all that is in them, but he rested on the seventh day. Therefore the LORD blessed the Sabbath day and made it holy.
[12] Honor your father and your mother, so that you may live long in the land the LORD your God is giving you.
[13] You shall not murder.
[14] You shall not commit adultery.
[15] You shall not steal.
[16] You shall not give false testimony against your neighbor.
[17] You shall not covet your neighbor's house. You shall not covet your neighbor's wife, or his manservant or maidservant, his ox or donkey, or anything that belongs to your neighbor.

The blessings of the law

There was also a blessing for them in obeying the law. In the book of Deuteronomy we find the Blessings that God promised to Israel on the condition that they were to obey the law.

Deuteronomy 28:1-14 NIV
[1] If you fully obey the LORD your God and carefully follow all his commands I give you today, the LORD your God will set you high above all the nations on earth. [2] All these blessings will come upon you and accompany you if you obey the LORD your God: [3] You will be blessed in the city and blessed in the country. [4] The fruit of your womb will be blessed, and the crops of your land and the young of your livestock-the calves of your herds and the lambs of your flocks. [5] Your basket and your kneading trough will be blessed. [6] You will be blessed when you come in and blessed when you go out. [7] The LORD will grant that the enemies who rise up against you will be defeated before you. They will come at you from one direction but flee from you in seven. [8] The LORD will send a blessing on your barns and on everything you put your hand to. The LORD your God will bless you in the land he is giving you. [9] The LORD will establish you as his holy people, as he promised you on oath, if you keep the commands of the LORD your God and walk in his ways. [10] Then all the peoples on earth will see that you are called by the name of the LORD, and they will fear you. [11] The LORD will grant you abundant prosperity-in the fruit of your womb, the young of your livestock and the crops of your ground-in the land he swore to your forefathers to give you. [12] The LORD will open the heavens, the storehouse of his bounty, to send rain on your land in season and to bless all the work of your hands. You will lend to many nations but will borrow from none. [13] The LORD will make you the head, not the tail. If you pay attention to the commands of the LORD your God that I give you this day and carefully follow them, you will always be at the top, never at the bottom. [14] Do not turn aside from any of the commands I give you today, to the right or to the left, following other gods and serving them.

A conditional blessing

The blessings of the law listed above were conditional to their obedience to the law. If they did not obey the law they were going to be under a curse. And the curses for disobedience were listed in Deuteronomy 28. I want you to take time and read through them and see how detrimental the curse was. When I was teaching on this subject in our church I took my time to read every verse, and the people's response was astounding. Reading through it will help you to understand why God sent Jesus to fulfil the Law and place us under Grace.

Deuteronomy 28:15-45 NIV

[15] However, if you do not obey the LORD your God and do not carefully follow all his commands and decrees I am giving you today, all these curses will come upon you and overtake you: [16] You will be cursed in the city and cursed in the country. [17] Your basket and your kneading trough will be cursed. [18] The fruit of your womb will be cursed, and the crops of your land, and the calves of your herds and the lambs of your flocks. [19] You will be cursed when you come in and cursed when you go out. [20] The LORD will send on you curses, confusion and rebuke in everything you put your hand to, until you are destroyed and come to sudden ruin because of the evil you have done in forsaking him. [21] The LORD will plague you with diseases until he has destroyed you from the land you are entering to possess. [22] The LORD will strike you with wasting disease, with fever and inflammation, with scorching heat and drought, with blight and mildew, which will plague you until you perish. [23] The sky over your head will be bronze, the ground beneath you iron. [24] The LORD will turn the rain of your country into dust and powder; it will come down from the skies until you are destroyed. [25] The LORD will cause you to be defeated before your enemies. You will come at them from one direction but flee from them in seven, and you will become a thing of horror to all the kingdoms on earth. [26] Your carcasses will be food for all the birds of the air and the beasts of the earth, and there will be no one to frighten them away. [27] The LORD will afflict you with the boils of Egypt and with tumors,

festering sores and the itch, from which you cannot be cured. [28] The LORD will afflict you with madness, blindness and confusion of mind. [29] At midday you will grope about like a blind man in the dark. You will be unsuccessful in everything you do; day after day you will be oppressed and robbed, with no one to rescue you. [30] You will be pledged to be married to a woman, but another will take her and ravish her. You will build a house, but you will not live in it. You will plant a vineyard, but you will not even begin to enjoy its fruit. [31] Your ox will be slaughtered before your eyes, but you will eat none of it. Your donkey will be forcibly taken from you and will not be returned. Your sheep will be given to your enemies, and no one will rescue them. [32] Your sons and daughters will be given to another nation, and you will wear out your eyes watching for them day after day, powerless to lift a hand. [33] A people that you do not know will eat what your land and labor produce, and you will have nothing but cruel oppression all your days. [34] The sights you see will drive you mad. [35] The LORD will afflict your knees and legs with painful boils that cannot be cured, spreading from the soles of your feet to the top of your head. [36] The LORD will drive you and the king you set over you to a nation unknown to you or your fathers. There you will worship other gods, gods of wood and stone. [37] You will become a thing of horror and an object of scorn and ridicule to all the nations where the LORD will drive you. [38] You will sow much seed in the field but you will harvest little, because locusts will devour it. [39] You will plant vineyards and cultivate them but you will not drink the wine or gather the grapes, because worms will eat them. [40] You will have olive trees throughout your country but you will not use the oil, because the olives will drop off. [41] You will have sons and daughters but you will not keep them, because they will go into captivity. [42] Swarms of locusts will take over all your trees and the crops of your land. [43] The alien who lives among you will rise above you higher and higher, but you will sink lower and lower. [44] He will lend to you, but you will not lend to him. He will be the head, but you will be the tail. [45] All these curses will come upon you. They will pursue you and overtake you until you are destroyed, because you did not obey the LORD your God and observe the commands and decrees he gave you.

Did you notice the number of curses listed for a person who makes a mistake under the law?

The failure of the law

The law was good, but a person had to keep the whole law in order to be righteous before God. If you broke one law, and you kept all the others, you were guilty of breaking the whole law. The law failed because one mistake breaks the whole law. The law made nothing perfect. The law brought sin-consciousness and not righteousness.

One mistake breaks the whole law

James 2:10-11
[10] For whoever keeps the whole law and yet stumbles at just one point is guilty of breaking all of it. [11] For he who said, "Do not commit adultery," also said, "Do not murder." If you do not commit adultery but do commit murder, you have become a lawbreaker.

The law made nothing perfect

Hebrews 7:18-19 AMP
[18] So a previous physical regulation and command is cancelled because of its weakness and ineffectiveness and uselessness—[19] For the Law never made anything perfect--but instead a better hope is introduced through which we [now] come close to God.

The law was ineffective. Instead of making people righteous, more people were guilty of breaking the law. There was no room for error. The soul who sinned had to die.

The law brought sin-consciousness

Romans 3:20 AMP
[20] For no person will be justified (made righteous, acquitted, and judged acceptable) in His sight by observing the works prescribed by the Law. For [the real function of] the Law is to make men recognize and be conscious of sin [not mere perception, but an acquaintance with sin which works toward repentance, faith, and holy character].

Instead of making us righteous, the law showed us how unrighteous we were.

God decided to send Jesus

It was at this point that God decided to send His son Jesus to come and fulfil the requirements of the Law and place us under His Grace. Please read the next verse attentively.

Galatians 4:4-5
[4] But when the fullness of the time had come, God sent forth His Son, born of a woman, born under the law, [5] to redeem those who were under the law, that we might receive the adoption as sons.

They thought Jesus broke the law

When Jesus came, the Jews did not understand His ministry. Everything He did was against the law according to them. In the book of John we read about Jesus coming to the pool of Bethesda on the Sabbath day and finding a man that had been paralysed for thirty-eight years. Jesus asked the man if he wanted to be well and he told Jesus that he had no one to put him into the water when the angel stirred the water. Jesus told him to pick up his bed and walk, and the man was healed immediately. The Jews saw him walking with his bed and they wanted to know why he was carrying his bed on a Sabbath day. He told them Jesus had healed him and told him to pick up his bed and walk. In the following verse we read that this was the reason why the Jews wanted to crucify Jesus, because according to them He broke the law.

John 5:16-18
[16] So, because Jesus was doing these things on the Sabbath, the Jews persecuted him. [17] Jesus said to them, "My Father is always at his work to this very day, and I, too, am working." [18] For this reason the Jews tried all the harder to kill him; not only was he breaking the Sabbath, but he was even calling God his own Father, making himself equal with God.

The Jews were furious that Jesus told the man to carry his bed on a Sabbath day. They wanted to crucify Him for that. Then He said He was the son of God, and that convinced them even more. Two things bothered them: 1) He said He was the son of God; 2) He broke the law by letting someone carry his bed on a Sabbath day. You would have expected them to be more compassionate about people than about rules and regulations, but they were not.

Jesus fulfilled the law

The Scribes and the Pharisees did not accept Jesus as the son of God, though He fulfilled all the prophecies. They also did not understand that He did not come to break the law but to fulfil it. Jesus said in **Matthew 5:17** *"Do not think that I have come to abolish the Law or the Prophets; I have not come to abolish them but to fulfill them."*

Jesus came to fulfil the law, not to break it. The Greek word for *fulfil* is the word *pleroo*. It means "to complete something, to accomplish or to bring to an end." Jesus came to complete the law. He accomplished the full requirements of the law, and He brought the law to an end.

Let me explain it to you in this manner. Imagine you are busy studying grade 11 and you get a teacher who comes and helps you with grade 11 maths, but he is actually a grade 12 teacher. He does not come to tell you to stop studying grade 11 maths; he is helping you to complete grade 11 so you can move on to grade 12. That's what Jesus came to do. He brought the Grace of God to us, but He helped us to fulfil the requirements of the Law so we can move on to Grace. We can't stay under the law forever. There is a higher level of spirituality. Therefore we read in **Romans 10:4** *"Christ is the end of the law so that there may be righteousness for everyone who believes."*

It does not mean when Jesus came He stopped the law. It simply means He took the law to the end and He ushered in a new thing called Grace. Jesus came to fulfil the requirements of the Law and then He introduced us to the Grace of God.

The new law

When Jesus had fulfilled the law, he ushered in the Grace of God. The Law came to an end through Him and Grace started with Him. God sent Him to close the old dispensation and open the new one. Jesus brought Grace and truth to us. The Apostle John explains it in the following verse:

John 1:17
[17] For the law was given through Moses, but grace and truth came through Jesus Christ.

Christ is the end of the law

Romans 10:4
[4] For Christ is the end of the law for righteousness to everyone who believes.

The Apostle Paul emphasised it further to let us know that Jesus has ended the Law. He brought the law to an end. He did not break it.

We are no longer under the law

Jesus redeemed us from the curse of the Law and we are now under Grace.

Romans 6:14
[14] For sin shall not have dominion over you, for you are not under law but under grace.

Sin will not hold you down anymore or block your way. God has forgiven all your past, present and future sin by Grace. Sin is eternally paid for. You have to receive God's forgiveness. This does not mean that everybody can just live in sin because their past and present sins are forgiven. You are free from sin and condemnation. I want you to continue reading and see what greater benefit the Grace of God will be to you.

The new commandment

Since we are no longer under the law, we have a new commandment. We are not lawless. We are still governed by a principle.

John 13:34
[34] A new commandment I give to you, that you love one another; as I have loved you, that you also love one another.

All the law is fulfilled in it

Galatians 5:14
[14] For all the law is fulfilled in one word, even in this: "You shall love your neighbor as yourself."

The new law that God has given us is love. Love fulfils the entire law. If you were to take the Ten Commandments and place them on one side and you take the new law of love and you place it on the other side you will realise that love has indeed replaced them all. If you walk in love you will automatically fulfil the entire law effortlessly. Instead of giving us a lot of *don'ts*, God has given us one *Do* that fulfils all the *Don'ts*.

The blessings of grace

Remember there was a Blessing for obedience to the Law. There is also a blessing under Grace. The difference between the Law and Grace is that the Law had a Blessing based on your obedience, but Grace is the unmerited favour of God that does not measure you according to your works. It is an unconditional Blessing. It was the Blessing that God had pronounced on Abraham. You are Abraham's seed and the Unconditional Blessing of Abraham is now upon you.

Galatians 3:13-14 NKJV
[13] Christ has redeemed us from the curse of the law, having become a curse for us (for it is written, "Cursed is everyone who hangs on a tree"), [14] that the blessing of Abraham might come upon the Gentiles in Christ Jesus, that we might receive the promise of the Spirit through faith.

Genesis 12:1-3 NKJV
[1] Now the LORD had said to Abram: "Get out of your country, From your family And from your father's house, To a land that I will show you. [2] I will make you a great nation; I will bless you And make your name great; And you shall be a blessing. [3] I will bless those who bless you, And I will curse him who curses you; And in you all the families of the earth shall be blessed."

You are not the seed of Moses, so do not claim the Blessing of the Law. Learn all the valuable lessons we can learn from Moses, but as far as the Blessing of the Law is concerned, it is not for you. The Blessing of Abraham is yours.

Grace is not a licence to sin

You may ask whether, since we are now under Grace, we can sin as much as we like and God will just forgive us. No, not at all. Grace is not a licence to sin. We are delivered from sin.

Romans 5:19-21

[19] For as by one man's disobedience many were made sinners, so also by one Man's obedience many will be made righteous. [20] Moreover the law entered that the offense might abound. But where sin abounded, grace abounded much more, [21] so that as sin reigned in death, even so grace might reign through righteousness to eternal life through Jesus Christ our Lord.

Romans 6:1-2

[1] What shall we say then? Shall we continue in sin that grace may abound? [2] Certainly not! How shall we who died to sin live any longer in it?

The Grace of God will empower you to live righteously. It does not cause you to indulge in sin.

Some used Grace as a licence to sin

In the times of the Apostles there were some people who used the Grace of God as a licence to sin. Jude, the brother of James, condemned their conduct in the verse below:

Jude 1:4

[4] For certain men have crept in unnoticed, who long ago were marked out for this condemnation, ungodly men, who turn the grace of our God into lewdness and deny the only Lord God and our Lord Jesus Christ.

Grace will cause you to deny ungodliness

Titus 2:11-13

[11] For the grace of God that brings salvation has appeared to all men, [12] teaching us that, denying ungodliness and worldly lusts, we should live soberly, righteously, and godly in the present age, [13] looking for the blessed hope and glorious appearing of our great God and Savior Jesus Christ.

Grace will make you say no to sin. Choose to deny ungodliness because God loves you so much. Choose to live right, not because you want to stand in your own righteousness but because you love God.

The benefits of grace

- If you sin there is forgiveness for you.
- Grace gives you boldness.
- Grace places you in right standing with God.

If you sin there is forgiveness for you

1 John 2:1
[1] My dear children, I write this to you so that you will not sin. But if anybody does sin, we have one who speaks to the Father in our defense--Jesus Christ, the Righteous One.

There is Grace for you if you sin. I want you to notice it does not say *when* you sin. It says *if* you sin. Which means it is there for when you make mistakes; you are not going to lose your blessing. God will forgive. It is also true that there are people who make deliberate mistakes. There is grace for you also. Let the Grace of God cause you to lay aside all sin and choose to live a life free from sin.

Grace gives you boldness

You no longer have to come to the throne of God weak, timid, unworthy and full of sin-consciousness. You can come with boldness and know all your sins are forgiven and God will grant all your requests.

Hebrews 4:16 AMP
[16] Let us then fearlessly and confidently and boldly draw near to the throne of grace (the throne of God's unmerited favor to us sinners), that we may receive mercy [for our failures] and find grace to help in good time for every need [appropriate help and well-timed help, coming just when we need it].

Grace places you in right standing with God

How would you feel if you knew that you are in right standing with God? You don't have to be like a child who is not sure whether their parent has forgiven their wrong. God sees you as righteous and He loves you unconditionally. You are not striving toward righteousness. You are righteous. You can stand before God and have no sense of guilt for any wrong you may have done, provided that you have repented.

Romans 3:24
[24] being justified freely by His grace through the redemption that is in Christ Jesus.

2 Corinthians 5:21
[21] For He made Him who knew no sin to be sin for us, that we might become the righteousness of God in Him.

No more condemnation

If you are in Christ you are a new creation; your old life has passed away and all things have become new. God has forgiven you the minute you asked for forgiveness for any sin you may have committed. You should receive your forgiveness in confidence and know you are forgiven. No matter if the consequences of your sin still remain; you were forgiven the minute you asked for forgiveness. No matter how you feel, you are forgiven.

Romans 8:1-2
[1] There is therefore now no condemnation to those who are in Christ Jesus, who do not walk according to the flesh, but according to the Spirit. [2] For the law of the Spirit of life in Christ Jesus has made me free from the law of sin and death.

You may have committed a sin that you can't easily erase from your memory. I want you to know that you are forgiven, no matter how severe that sin may be. God has forgiven you. You don't have to beg for God's forgiveness every time you come into His presence. He has forgiven you. Any form of condemnation you may still feel is from satan. Condemnation is never from God. You are free from the law of sin and death. Hallelujah.

CHAPTER 8

PROSPERITY

3 John 1:2-3 NKJV
[2] Beloved, I pray that you may prosper in all things and be in health, just as your soul prospers. [3] For I rejoiced greatly when brethren came and testified of the truth that is in you, just as you walk in the truth.

Throughout the Bible God has promised his servants prosperity. God promised Abraham that He will bless him and make his name great and bless all the nations of the earth through him. To be blessed means to be prosperous.

God also promised Israel to take them to a land flowing with milk and honey. Milk and honey in the Bible are referred to as the good life. It is synonymous of a prosperous life.

Prosperity means to live a comfortable life of peace and abundance. It means to lack nothing. To have all your needs met. It means to be able to give to others as much as they need without creating a lack on your side.

Before we can discuss prosperity, it is important for us to determine scripturally if God wants His children to be prosperous. It will be of no value for us to discuss prosperity and not believe it is for us. If we are in doubt whether God wants us to be prosperous we will have no prosperity at all, because a double-minded man will not receive anything from God.

The word *prosperity* has caused a lot of controversy in the church of the Lord Jesus Christ. Many Christians believe they should live in poverty so they can remain humble and dependent on God. This is not true, but maybe some of them need to live in poverty.

The question is: "Does God want us to prosper?"

We will now look at scriptural references to see whether God wants us prosperous or not. I want you to read the verses below so you can come to a biblical conclusion whether God wants you poor or prosperous.

➢ Financial prosperity is part of the finished work of the cross

2 Corinthians 8:9
[9] For you know the grace of our Lord Jesus Christ, that though He was rich, yet for your sakes He became poor, that you through His poverty might become rich.

It is clear in the above scripture that Jesus became poor that we might be rich. Wealth is part of what Jesus has purchased for us on the cross. It is a gift by grace.

➢ Prosperity is God's plan for your life

Jeremiah 29:11 NIV
[11] "For I know the plans I have for you," declares the Lord, "plans to prosper you and not to harm you, plans to give you hope and a future."

➢ The blessing of the Lord makes one rich

Proverbs 10:22
[22] The blessing of the LORD makes one rich, And He adds no sorrow with it.

According to the above verse, riches are a sign of the blessing in the life of a born again Christian.

➢ God gives the ability to get wealth

Deuteronomy 8:18
[18] And you shall remember the LORD your God, for it is He who gives you power to get wealth, that He may establish His covenant which He swore to your fathers, as it is this day.

If prosperity is not from God, then why did He give us the ability to get wealth? Can you imagine God giving you eyes and then telling you not to look through them because there are many temptations in the world? In the same way, God has given us the ability to get wealth to do the right things. There are people who do wrong with wealth, but you will do right with wealth.

➢ Jesus instructed us to give so we can have abundance

Luke 6:38
[38] Give, and it will be given to you: good measure, pressed down, shaken together, and running over will be put into your bosom. For with the same measure that you use, it will be measured back to you.

There is no way you can give financially in the kingdom of God and stay poor.

➤ When you walk in the fear of the Lord, wealth and riches will be in your house

Psalm 112:3
[3] Wealth and riches will be in his house, And his righteousness endures forever.

➤ All things are added unto you in the kingdom of God

Matthew 6:31-33
[31] Therefore do not worry, saying, "What shall we eat?" or "What shall we drink?" or "What shall we wear?" [32] For after all these things the Gentiles seek. For your heavenly Father knows that you need all these things. [33] But seek first the kingdom of God and His righteousness, and all these things shall be added to you.

The wealth of the wicked is laid up for the righteous

Proverbs 13:22
[22] A good man leaves an inheritance to his children's children, But the wealth of the sinner is stored up for the righteous.

Job 27:16-17
[16] Though he heaps up silver like dust, And piles up clothing like clay—[17] He may pile it up, but the just will wear it, And the innocent will divide the silver.

God gave engineers, designers and architects the ability to design beautiful houses, buildings, cars and clothes; not so that the sinners can have it. The job of the sinners is to gather the wealth so it can come to you, the rightful owner.

In the above scriptures it is clear to see, without explanation, that it is impossible for a Christian to give, to seek the kingdom of God, to fear the Lord, to have the blessing of God, and to follow the plan of God, yet remain poor. There are too many ways in which God has purposed to channel riches to His children. One must be naive and wilfully stubborn to read these verses and still not believe in financial prosperity.

God delights in the prosperity of His servants

Psalm 35:27
[27] Let them shout for joy and be glad, Who favor my righteous cause; And let them say continually, "Let the LORD be magnified, Who has pleasure in the prosperity of His servant."

It brings God joy to see His children prospering. He wants to see His children blessed, just like any other parent wants to see his children prosperous.

Myths about prosperity

Prosperity is from the devil

In the book of Job the devil admitted that God made Job rich and had given him an easy life. When the devil started to attack Job, he attacked the prosperity of Job. If the devil makes people prosperous, why did he make Job poor?

You must be poor to go to heaven

God blessed Abraham and made him rich. Why would God make the father of our faith rich if the wealth was going to keep him out of heaven?

Jesus said it is difficult for a rich man to enter into the kingdom of heaven. He did not say rich men do not go to heaven. He was referring to the sense of independence and superiority that money gives to a rich man.

Are Christians supposed to be rich?

Abraham is our father in the faith and he was very rich

Genesis 13:2
[2] Abram was very rich in livestock, in silver, and in gold.

King David was considered to be a rich man

2 Samuel 12:2
[2] The rich man had exceedingly many flocks and herds.

The disciples were prosperous and able to help those in need

Acts 11:29 AMP
[29] So the disciples resolved to send relief, each according to his individual ability [in proportion as he had prospered], to the brethren who lived in Judea.

Money is a tool

Money solves many problems, but we must serve God and not money.

Money answers all things

Ecclesiastes 10:19
[19] A feast is made for laughter, And wine makes merry; But money answers everything.

Money is the common language that is understood around the world when it comes to the exchange of goods and services. An unsaved landlord will not necessarily give space to a saved Christian just because they are Christian. He will rent space to a person who has the money. If Christians believe money is evil, they will always be reduced to beggars and bad payers.

There are too many places where Christians are refused services because they have built a reputation of not paying their rent or debts. Many Christians are blacklisted and bankrupt. The problem is they hate prosperity. When you hate prosperity you will not be prosperous. You will always have lack and shortage. How can you hate prosperity but you also want to buy a car, a house, food and rent buildings? I am not saying you should start loving money and become materialistic. The love of money is the root of evil. I am suggesting you see money for what God has intended it to be; a tool to open many things that are locked up.

You can build the kingdom of God

The sad thing about the church is that most business people do not trust churches. You would think that the church should be the institution that instils the most trust when it comes to financial integrity, but it is not always the case. Landlords of corporate buildings and rental companies will rather rent a space to a new business before they consider a five-year-old church. The church has become known for not paying because they have taken on big rental payments in the name of faith and neglected to pay, without making arrangements or communicating in time to their landlords.

If the church has more money, it has more muscle to buy buildings, land and equipment to preach the gospel and to reach more souls. A church that is able to reach more people with the gospel is a church that has financial resources to fund the preaching of the gospel. Many churches are renting buildings because they are struggling to buy property or build their own buildings. Some churches are even going on sale and they are sold to private investors for business because the church cannot afford to buy them. Most of this tragedy was caused because some churches thought that prosperity was not for Christians. Prosperity is for us! God gives us the ability to get wealth to establish His covenant on the earth. You need to be rich so you can fund the gospel.

The negative side of money

Money is a great tool that will help you require the necessary goods and services for life and living. Just as money can solve many problems and open many doors, it can also cause an innumerable number of problems. That is why many people have decided not to be rich, and there is nothing wrong with that decision. It keeps them from danger and it gives a purpose to life. Can you imagine a world where everybody was rich? Who will build roads and collect garbage? Who will sweep floors and work on motor car engines? It is also important to note that it is not necessarily money that is causing challenges, but your relationship with money. If you can learn to relate well with money, you can be prosperous and a kingdom financier. I want to share with you here below a few pitfalls regarding prosperity. If you can avoid them you can become a Joseph of Arimathea in the kingdom of God.

Prosperity can make you less dependent on God

Money can give a person a false sense of security. You may or may not have noticed that miracles are more prevalent among the poor. It is because poor people don't have money to consult doctors and buy medication. When they receive the gospel message regarding healing, it is many times their only hope for healing. Their circumstances have also shown them that nothing is impossible with God. It is for this reason that you sometimes hear those who are ignorant saying that Pastors are exploiting poor people when they preach the gospel to them and receive offerings. What they don't know is that poor people have a heart for God and God has a heart for poor people. Preachers who preach to the poor have the compassion of God for His people. Most preachers would rather preach to rich people if it was about money, but they have learnt that money is not everything.

A rich person might easily resort to tablets and doctors' consultations, because they have the money. That is why Jesus said that as hard as it is for a camel to go through the eye of a needle, so hard will it be for a rich man to enter into the kingdom of heaven. It will be hard because money can easily replace your faith. That is why some Christians don't want money; they know they won't be able to stay faithful to God. I think it is good as long as they realise that there are other people who can have a lot of money and still trust God and remain faithful. Isaac was rich and he did not forget God. Let the abundance of money rather make you a kingdom financier and not an idol worshipper. Open your purse toward the gospel.

Money is an amplifier

Have you ever had friends who were the most humble people when they did not have money, but when they got money you couldn't believe how they changed toward you? Money has the ability to amplify the character, desires and thoughts of a person. A glutton will eat more when he has money; his poverty will keep him slim. A proud person will show off their pride when they have money; poverty kept them humble. In both situations it is not the money that produced the spirit of pride or the spirit of gluttony. Money just amplified a problem that already existed. Be careful how you act toward people who were there for you when you did not have money. Don't change and treat them badly. Be appreciative, thankful and humble.

The love of money is the root of evil

1 Timothy 6:10
[10] For the love of money is a root of all kinds of evil, for which some have strayed from the faith in their greediness, and pierced themselves through with many sorrows.

I want you to notice that the Apostle Paul said, *"For the love of money is a root of all kinds of evil."* He did not say *money* is the root of evil. Have you noticed? I have heard many people, even Christians, saying in social circles, "Money is the root of evil." Please take care to read this scripture to avoid error. Jesus told the Pharisees, *"You err because you don't know the scriptures."*

The love of money can cause you to make hasty decisions. You have to fight and destroy the spirit of financial greed. The love of money will destroy your discernment and cause you to invest money in anything that glitters. It will cause you to sacrifice your family just to chase after money. It will cause you to sacrifice your marriage and rather go for more money. If you love money, you will never have enough.

Money can be an idol

Matthew 6:24
[24] No one can serve two masters; for either he will hate the one and love the other, or else he will be loyal to the one and despise the other. You cannot serve God and mammon.

There are people who have made money their God. They will lie, steal, kill, stay out of church, and sacrifice their family just to make money. To such a person money has become their god. It was for this reason that Ananias and Sapphira were killed in the New Testament after they kept a portion of the money they were supposed to give to God. Money became an idol to them and the judgement of God fell on them. Don't let money become your god. If you have to choose between giving your tithes to God or spending it on worldly comfort, rather choose to give to God.

The love of money can destroy good relationships

Many families, marriages and relationships have been destroyed by people's imbalanced chase after money. Some have gone to work in faraway places only to find on their return that their family is scattered or they have grown apart. Others have taken on extra jobs and overtime shifts to make more money to provide for the family, only to realise their children became hooked on substances and their spouses have fallen in adultery while they were so focused on making more money for the family. Don't chase success and the things of this world at the cost of good relationships. Rather stay in an average neighbourhood and drive an average car than staying in that upmarket neighbourhood with you fancy car with nobody in the passenger seat and no one behind the designer door of that big house to welcome you home. Don't chase prosperity at the cost of your relationships. There is nothing money can buy to replace loneliness. Loneliness is solved by good relationships and not by material things.

Man is never satisfied

How much money do you think will ever be enough for you? The answer to that question might be different for everybody. The truth is that man is never satisfied. Nothing can satisfy the human soul except the Spirit and the Word of God. A person may buy their dream car today and in a few months or years realise they want a car with a bit more features and luxury. Possessions cannot satisfy the human soul. As long as man has eyes to see things and a mind to imagine, he will rarely be satisfied, unless he finds his satisfaction in God.

Proverbs 27:20
[20] Hell and Destruction are never full; So the eyes of man are never satisfied.

The purpose of prosperity

Let us now look at the purpose of prosperity; the reason why God gives us wealth.

➢ To glorify God

God is not glorified by your poverty. When you are prosperous, your prosperity can become a testimony that will inspire many others. There was a time when nobody wanted to become a pastor because they thought pastors were poor people. Then, in the twentieth century, even news reporters said they wanted to become pastors because you can get rich overnight. They obviously did not mean it in a good way, but I want you to realise that Pastors have become synonymous with prosperity. However, I want you to know that you don't have to become a pastor to be prosperous. You need to be a Christian. God wants to make you a showpiece of His goodness. God wants to make you an infomercial of heaven's benefits. God wants your clothes, your car, your house, your shoes and whatever you desire to become a living testimony of His glory. There might be people who are annoyed when Christians are prosperous but I want you to know that God is glorified when His children are prosperous. Look at the verse below.

John 15:7-8
[7] If you abide in Me, and My words abide in you, you will ask what you desire, and it shall be done for you. [8] By this My Father is glorified, that you bear much fruit; so you will be My disciples.

➢ **To establish God's covenant**

The highest heavens belong to the Lord but He has given the earth to the sons of men. God wants His children to dominate the earth. As the people of God we have to take charge of the earth. We are going to need finances to take charge of the earth. It is not a blessing for a church to rent a piece of land in a world your God created for you. It is clear in the verse below that God will give us wealth to establish His covenant.

Deuteronomy 8:18
[18] And you shall remember the LORD your God, for it is He who gives you power to get wealth, that He may establish His covenant which He swore to your fathers, as it is this day.

As a child of God you need to see your job or business as a gift and opportunity from God to fund His kingdom. You need to become a kingdom financier.

➢ To fund the gospel

Luke 8:1-3
[1] Now it came to pass, afterward, that He went through every city and village, preaching and bringing the glad tidings of the kingdom of God. And the twelve were with Him, [2] and certain women who had been healed of evil spirits and infirmities--Mary called Magdalene, out of whom had come seven demons, [3] and Joanna the wife of Chuza, Herod's steward, and Susanna, and many others who provided for Him from their substance.

There is a need for kingdom financiers to fund the gospel. The ministry of Jesus was supported by certain women who had benefited from His anointing. They also gathered influential women to use their wealth to fund the ministry of Jesus.

➢ To support those who are preaching the gospel so they can give themselves to prayer for the benefit of the people of God

The level of the anointing on the preacher is determined by the dedication of the preacher to prayer. The greater the anointing on the preacher, the more successful the members will be. A prayerful preacher has a greater anointing to destroy the works of the devil. The Apostles devoted themselves to prayer and to the study of the Word. Their ministry was marked by miracles, and nobody had lack among them.

I believe it is not wrong for a preacher to work a daily job and provide for his family, provided that he spends a reasonable time in prayer and the study of the Word. What I have also noticed is that when a preacher is financially provided for, he can spend time studying the Word and praying and become more successful spiritually. When a preacher's anointing increases, his income also increases. Prayer and the study of the Word increase your anointing. Prayer is the number one job of the preacher. The success of the ministry depends on prayer.

Acts 6:3-4
[3] Therefore, brethren, seek out from among you seven men of good reputation, full of the Holy Spirit and wisdom, whom we may appoint over this business; [4] but we will give ourselves continually to prayer and to the ministry of the word.

➤ To provide for the preachers

Just as normal people work a daily job for an income, a preacher also has to receive an income when he preaches the gospel. The problem is that many people feel that preachers should suffer. God has ordained that preachers make a living from the income of the church. I am not scared to tell my congregation I receive an income from what they are giving in the church. I think it is a disgrace for a preacher to boast and say his business is supporting him and not the church. That sounds good to your critics, but God has ordained it that you receive and income from the tithes and offerings so the blessing that He places upon you as a preacher can pass onto His people. The anointing flows from the top down. I would not want to be a member of a church where the pastor is his own provider.

1 Corinthians 9:14
[14] Even so the Lord has commanded that those who preach the gospel should live from the gospel.

Galatians 6:6
[6] Let him who is taught the word share in all good things with him who teaches.

➤ To finance the vision of God and to fund the truth

Matthew 28:11-16
[11] Now while they were going, behold, some of the guard came into the city and reported to the chief priests all the things that had

happened. [12] When they had assembled with the elders and consulted together, they gave a large sum of money to the soldiers, [13] saying, "Tell them, 'His disciples came at night and stole Him away while we slept.' [14] And if this comes to the governor's ears, we will appease him and make you secure." [15] So they took the money and did as they were instructed; and this saying is commonly reported among the Jews until this day. [16] Then the eleven disciples went away into Galilee, to the mountain which Jesus had appointed for them.

The media is a powerful tool of influence in the world. You can decide to spread a lie and be successful. If there are two people, one telling the truth and the other telling a lie, people will not necessarily believe the truth just because the one had the truth. People will believe the most convincing one of the two. The only way you can become convincing is when you have the resources to teach people constantly through the media. Man is a product of what he is told. If you tell a person a lie over and over again they will eventually believe it. We need finances to spread the gospel. We need to tell it over and over again in order to stop the lies the world wants to spread through the media.

God's word is truth and the truth needs to spread to all men. At the crucifixion of Jesus they financed a lie, but as the church we need to finance the truth. The only reason why lies are increasing is because the truth is not published. Are you currently financing a lie or the truth?

➢ To provide for the poor

The work of the church is to preach the gospel and make disciples of all nations. We are not a charitable organisation but at times we might do charitable work. As we preach the gospel we may also encounter poverty and lack. When the church is financially strong it can somehow help the poor as the Apostles did in the book of Acts.

➤ **To buy property for the church**

A poor church cannot buy or maintain a piece of property. One day I was so upset with a church that had an expensive frame tent structure that was wasting away in the sun and rain. The tent sails were torn and the once beautiful stage was broken down. Children were playing in the sanctuary during the day. The church abandoned the structure to have church meetings in the pastor's garage. As I stood there and looked at the once beautiful structure with anger in my spirit, the Holy Spirit later whispered to me that they don't have money to maintain the tent. I was stunned. The church needs finances to buy property and maintain it. We need people who will be like David who would say, *"I will surely buy it from you for a price; nor will I offer burnt offerings to the LORD my God with that which costs me nothing."*

2 Samuel 24:24
[24] Then the king said to Araunah, "No, but I will surely buy it from you for a price; nor will I offer burnt offerings to the LORD my God with that which costs me nothing." So David bought the threshing floor and the oxen for fifty shekels of silver.

How to unlock your prosperity

It is very simple to unlock prosperity in your live. There are only two things. First of all you have to believe in prosperity because you will believe what you receive, and secondly you have to be a tither. A non-tither has a curse upon their life. Trying to be prosperous while you are cursed is an impossible task. So it would be best for you to break the curse first to unlock the blessing.

• **Believe**

You will never receive what you do not believe. A double-minded man will not receive anything from God. Without Faith it is impossible to receive anything from God. Your faith is the starting point for receiving anything from God. If you still have to reason whether God wants you poor or rich, you are very far from the road to the blessing.

In the same manner, if your preacher does not believe in prosperity, you will not live in prosperity. The minute you hear your preacher is against prosperity preachers you should know he is standing for poverty preachers. The ironic thing of the church is that some Christians think they can speak against healing, yet have divine health when they are sick. They think they can speak against prophets, yet have fulfilment of prophecies. Some think they can speak against prosperity, yet live in prosperity. God is not mocked – a man shall reap whatsoever he sows. God will not give you something you criticise.

• Money and faith

True faith can produce money, but faith itself is not money. You have to use your faith to speak money into existence, speak a job into existence, and speak prosperity over your business. There are people who function in foolishness and call it faith. They will sign a contract to rent a R3 000 building while their total income is R4 000. That is foolishness and not faith.

• Tithe

Your tithe opens the floodgates of heaven. It is so sad to see many people in a prayer line asking for prayer for a financial miracle. To me they are like a farmer who has not planted a seed and he is sitting on his porch asking God for rain. Weeds will grow when it rains. That is the struggle many non-tithing Christians are facing. They do not tithe and they are under a financial curse. They read the verse and close the Bible and expect a different result from what they have read the Bible says will happen to non-tithers. Look at this verse again.

Malachi 3:9-12

[9] "You are cursed with a curse, For you have robbed Me, Even this whole nation. [10] Bring all the tithes into the storehouse, That there may be food in My house, And try Me now in this," Says the LORD of hosts, "If I will not open for you the windows of heaven And pour out for you such blessing That there will not be room enough to receive it. [11] And I will rebuke the devourer for your sakes, So that he will not destroy the fruit of your ground, Nor shall the vine fail to bear fruit for you in the field," Says the LORD of hosts; [12] "And all nations will call you blessed, For you will be a delightful land," Says the LORD of hosts.

Decide to break the curse upon your life through faith and tithing and start walking in the blessing of the Lord that will make you rich and add no sorrow to your life.

CHAPTER 9

BLESSED BEYOND THE CURSE

Galatians 3:13-14 NKJV

[13] Christ has redeemed us from the curse of the law, having become a curse for us (for it is written, "Cursed is everyone who hangs on a tree"), [14] that the blessing of Abraham might come upon the Gentiles in Christ Jesus, that we might receive the promise of the Spirit through faith.

No Christian should live under fear of a curse or being cursed. As a child of God, the curse is broken in your life.

All mankind was under a curse because of the fall of Adam, but we were redeemed from the curse by the death and resurrection of Jesus Christ. I want you to notice that the curse is broken, but the benefit of the blessing is not automatic. You have to receive the blessing of Abraham by faith. The blessing of Abraham will cause you to be prosperous and fruitful in every area of your life. It will restore your flesh and refresh your body.

What I mean is that though Christ has redeemed us from the curse, it is still possible for a person to live under the curse instead of living under the blessing.

In this chapter we will look at the different kinds of curses God has delivered us from and how we can lay hold of our freedom and live in the Blessing. I want you to know that all of the different kinds of curses are also collectively referred to as the Curse of the Law. In the book of Deuteronomy 28 we read the collection of curses that was under the law.

What is a curse?

A curse is a declaration of evil over a person that will **hinder** his **progress**, **affect** his **health** and **steal** his **joy** in life. It can also be the consequences of disobedience.

The cause of a curse

Proverbs 26:2 NKJV
[2] Like a flitting sparrow, like a flying swallow, So a curse without cause shall not alight.

A curse does not just automatically fall on a person. There must be a cause for a curse. The following are the most common causes for curse:

- Disobedience (sin)
- Anger
- Jealousy
- Fear
- Dishonour

➢ Disobedience

Through Adam's disobedience, all mankind was under a curse. If a person still walks in disobedience today, they walk under the curse of the law.

➢ Anger

Some parents might curse their children out of anger. One person may curse another out of anger caused by an argument or disagreement. A teacher might curse a child out of anger by telling the child, "You will never get anywhere in life; you are stupid."

➢ Jealousy

A curse of jealousy is when someone becomes jealous of the progress of another. Such a curse is caused by greed. If a person progresses too fast in the workplace, his colleagues might become jealous of them and try anything in their power to block their way. A person's neighbour might be jealous of their progress and try and block their way.

➢ Fear

The curse that is caused by fear is also called a self-inflicted curse. A person might walk in fear and bring a curse upon them. You find a person might walk in constant fear that they might contract a certain disease that is working havoc in their family. The person might fear that they will contract cancer or end up divorced as all their family members. There are Christians who walk in constant fear that others will hold their blessings back. They believe more in the power of darkness than believing in God. Such curses are self-inflicted.

➤ **Dishonour**

When you dishonour authority you are under a curse. All authority has been given by God. Ham was cursed because he exposed his father's nakedness. When a person dishonours a Man of God, they are cursed. When you dishonour your parents, you are cursed.

Wherever there is a curse you can trace it back to one of the above offences.

Different kinds of curses

- The curse of the law
- Bloodline curses
- Self-inflicted curses
- The curse of the prophets
- Financial curses
- The curse of men

The curse of the law is the result of disobedience. Bloodline curses are the result of disobedience.

• **The curse of the Law**

The curse of the law is caused by disobedience. A person who is walking in sin is under the curse of the law.

Romans 5:12,17,19 NKJV
[12] Therefore, just as through one man sin entered the world, and death through sin, and thus death spread to all men, because all sinned- [17] For if by the one man's offense death reigned through the one, much more those who receive abundance of grace and of the gift of righteousness will reign in life through the One, Jesus Christ. [19] For as by one man's disobedience many were made sinners, so also by one Man's obedience many will be made righteous.

Through the fall of Adam all mankind was under the curse of the law. But through the death and resurrection of our Lord Jesus Christ the curse was broken. Christ has redeemed us from the curse of the law. By becoming born again you move out under the curse of the Law.

Under the Law a person was cursed coming in and cursed going out. Jesus blessed our coming and going out.

The curse of the Law is broken by the born-again experience

2 Corinthians 5:17
[17] Therefore, if anyone is in Christ, he is a new creation; old things have passed away; behold, all things have become new.

Through the born-again experience we are no longer in Adam. Christ has redeemed us from Adam. Jesus did not come to restore to us what Adam had lost. We are not a revived Adam. We are born after the second Adam who is Jesus Christ. We are no longer in Adam but in Christ. You do not have an Adamic nature; you have the divine nature. You might have flesh like Adam but the curse of Adam is broken over your life.

• Bloodline curses

It simply means whatever sicknesses, wickedness, destructions and hindrances were on a person's family will come upon them. This curse is found in Exodus 20.

Exodus 20:5
[5] you shall not bow down to them nor serve them. For I, the LORD your God, am a jealous God, visiting the iniquity of the fathers upon the children to the third and fourth generations of those who hate Me.

This is the main verse that is upheld by those who teach and propagate bloodline curses. Many Christians did not worry about curses when they were sinners, but the minute they are born again they begin to study curses. The truth is, when you become born again every curse is broken.

Bloodline curses are curses that are the result of your family heritage. These curses can be generational diseases that run in a certain family. When a person goes to the doctor, the doctor might do a premedical history check through direct questioning. At times you might be requested to fill up a medical questionnaire containing direct questions on specific ailments that might be related to your family. The reasoning behind it is that if a certain sickness runs in your family, you might also be more prone to suffer from it in future.

You find that some families are plagued by cancer, diabetes, multiple sclerosis, sexual sins or alcoholism. Other families might struggle to hold their marriages together. You might find that in such a family many of their marriages failed.

The curse is broken

The good news is you don't have to fear anymore. You don't have to feel helpless thinking you are going to attract a disease or any form of misfortune that runs in your family. There is good news for you; just continue reading.

Jeremiah 31:29-32 NKJV
[29] In those days they shall say no more: "The fathers have eaten sour grapes, And the children's teeth are set on edge. [30] But every one shall die for his own iniquity; every man who eats the sour grapes, his teeth shall be set on edge. [31] Behold, the days are coming, says the LORD, when I will make a new covenant with the house of Israel and with the house of Judah—[32] not according to the covenant that I made with their fathers in the day that I took them by the hand to lead them out of the land of Egypt, My

covenant which they broke, though I was a husband to them, says the LORD."

In this verse we see that God has promised to break the curse of the fathers over the children, so it would be unscriptural for someone to believe that they are still suffering the sins of their father.

Nobody will have a curse bestowed upon them that they have no control over. People who believe in bloodline curses believe that it is just the way it is and the person who suffers a bloodline curse can do nothing about it. It is just bestowed upon them. The curse of the fathers is broken over the children. The child might follow the father because he was exposed to the sins of the father, but it will not be a bloodline curse. The child will do it out of their own choice. This verse says each person's teeth will be set on edge because they themselves have eaten sour grapes.

Delivered from your bloodline curses

1 Peter 1:17-19 NKJV
[17] And if you call on the Father, who without partiality judges according to each one's work, conduct yourselves throughout the time of your stay here in fear; [18] knowing that you were not redeemed with corruptible things, like silver or gold, from your aimless conduct received by tradition from your fathers, [19] but with the precious blood of Christ, as of a lamb without blemish and without spot.

Bloodline and family curses are a reality if you are unsaved. It is also possible that a born again believer can still experience the effects of bloodline curses in his life because of ignorance or fear. We were all born into sin by virtue of our natural birth. Through this natural birth we are connected to our biological parenthood with Adam as our ancient forefather and we are therefore heirs of their bloodline. **1 Peter 1:18** says *"We received an empty way of life handed down from our forefathers."* Indeed, if some of us should go down our family tree all we will find are witches, sickness, drunkards, slaves, adulterers, fornicators and sinners. Adam himself was a cursed man and whoever still hails from him is a shareholder of the curse.

I feel the need to mention this to you although it is of no profit to me. I studied demonology and bloodline curses in the early stages of my ministry. I had stacks of textbooks on all sorts of topics concerning curses. I have read most books about bloodline curses, demons and the testimonies of those who were once sold-out satanists but are now born again believers. I was doing deliverance sessions as well, until God opened my eyes to the finished work of the cross and the inheritance that we Christians have by the death of Jesus Christ.

Christ redeemed us from the curse of the law, through the death of the cross. No Christian can say they are still under a curse or being cursed. The curse may only function in your life due to ignorance, fear and unbelief. Through salvation you have been transferred from bloodline curses to bloodline blessings. You are no longer under the bloodline of your family, but under the blood of Jesus. You've got to lay hold of the blessing by faith.

If you still notice the effect of family curses in your life I want you to disconnect yourself from it and break it in Jesus name. A bloodline curse is caused by ignorance, fear or disobedience. A person might be ignorant of the fact that Jesus has redeemed them from the curse, and it will function in their life. Another might fear that they will suffer the same disease that is working havoc in their family and it might come upon them because of fear. Walking in disobedience through sin can open the door for a person to function under a curse.

Once you receive salvation, you have become a new creation in Christ and every curse is broken in your life. Deliverance from curses is part of the package of salvation. The Greek word for *salvation* is *soteria* which includes deliverance and redemption. You are therefore delivered and redeemed from the curse. You are no longer connected to the natural infirmities of your family lineage. You are no longer under bloodline curses but under bloodline blessings. The blessing of Abraham is upon you. Believe it and declare it over your life.

• Self-inflicted curses

Many people have accepted curses into their lives ignorantly. Others have tried to progress in life but they keep seeing themselves returning to the same point. Some would say they have never believed in a curse but they have been struggling for the past years now and therefore they have begun to wonder if they are not under a curse. Many times it is because they do the same things over and over again and expect a different result, so out of ignorance they claim curses. You find many Christians don't have enough faith in God and they go to sangomas or spiritual witch-doctors who portray themselves as ministers of the gospel and who tell them they are under a curse. Some people never really build their faith. They try everything from the sense realm. It is easy for such people to return to witches. They go to fortune tellers where they are told many half-truths and they believe it and think their Pastor is unspiritual and he did not see it.

What those spirits do most of the time is they alienate the person from people they are supposed to believe. They will tell them, "Your Pastor is blocking your blessings" or, "Your family member is busy with you." They will tell you, "Your colleague is standing in your way of progress at work." They will turn people against their neighbours. Their aim is to alienate you from people you are supposed to trust so they can lead you by your nose in any direction they want you to go.

Curses inflicted by ignorance

Many believers fall prey to the devil because of their ignorance. They receive Christ as their saviour but they make no effort to know what salvation is all about. Others are just plain lazy to study the Bible. Your ignorance can cost you greatly.

Hosea 4:6

[6] My people are destroyed for lack of knowledge. Because you have rejected knowledge, I also will reject you from being priest for Me; Because you have forgotten the law of your God, I also will forget your children.

If you are born again, a curse cannot function in your life unless you allow it. Many Christians are victims of curses because they have silently accepted that it is their family heritage. Their ignorance of the fact that the curse is broken has made them open to the curse.

Curses inflicted by words

A curse can be inflicted by words that are spoken over your life.

Proverbs 18:21

[21] Death and life are in the power of the tongue, And those who love it will eat its fruit.

Some people are speaking curses over themselves the whole day. Their conversations are filled with curses. They continuously confess: "I am sick. I will not make it. I am poor. I don't have money. I am dying to hear from you. These shoes are killing me." Those are all phrases that are casually swung around by ignorant people who think they are just speaking figuratively. The truth is that you are speaking negative words over yourself whether it is literally or figuratively. Those are self-inflicted curses. You have to learn to speak theright words over yourself.

Resist the devil

Even if you begin to see the signs of the presence of a curse in your life you have to deliberately decide to resist the devil, and he will flee from you. You can't just lie there and accept all kinds of curses in your life. You will have to take authority over your life and cast the devil out. Don't agree with the negative you are seeing at work in your life. Arm yourself with the word of God and break every curse. Keep declaring nobody can curse me. I am free from the curse. I am blessed. Refuse to believe anything else. You are going to have to fight for what you want. Fight the good fight of faith. It is an easy fight.

• The curse of the prophets

There is what we refer to as the curse of the Prophets. This is a curse that comes upon a person when they dishonour a servant of God. This curse does not come upon people because the Prophet has cursed them. No. This curse is from God for dishonouring His servant. You should have respect for those whom God has called to carry His name. Whether you agree with them or their way of ministry is irrelevant. Don't place yourself in the line of fire by trying to be a judge over God's servants; you might bring the curse of the Prophets over yourself. Do not touch the Lord's anointed.

Psalm 105:14-16

[14] He permitted no one to do them wrong; Yes, He rebuked kings for their sakes, [15] Saying, "Do not touch My anointed ones, And do My prophets no harm." [16] Moreover He called for a famine in the land; He destroyed all the provision of bread.

We live in a world that has lost respect for ministers of the gospel. They feel a righteous anger toward ministers of the gospel. Some have taken the position of spiritual guardians in the body of Christ, to protect God's people from whom they believe is being a false prophet. They address Men of God with disrespect. I have been in a meeting once where even ministers of the gospel referred to someone as a little boy, because they labelled him to be a false prophet. They disregarded the Man of God for his age and because they did not agree with his line of ministry. I was so grieved in my spirit. I was astonished that even some ministers of the gospel were not properly trained in the things of the Spirit to know you should not dishonour another Man of God.

What most Pastors don't realise is that in the same way you discredit other ministers of the gospel in front of your church members, you are teaching them to discredit you when they don't agree with you. I have seen many Pastors suffering persecution in their own ministries and losing what once was an ideal church because they have spoken against ministers of the gospel.

We should learn a lot from the story of David and Saul. After God had rejected Saul as king and chosen David as the next king, Saul was chasing David to kill him. Saul was totally wrong, but David still honoured Saul as the Lord's anointed. How can you then dishonour someone whom God has not rejected? You have rejected the person because you don't understand their way of doing ministry? Be careful, you might bring the curse of the Prophet upon yourself. God Himself will defend His servant.

Most people who call other ministers of the gospel false prophets do so because of something they have read in newspapers or seen on social media. How can you label someone to be a false prophet after you have seen a social media posting? Should you not have seen it after you have read the word of God? Should you not be led by the Bible and not by newspapers and social media postings? Since when has the worldly system become a source of discernment for the church? Don't be led by a worldly system; be led by the Spirit and the Word of God.

Be afraid to touch the Lord's anointed

You should have a holy fear that is based on respect when it comes to ministers of the gospel. You should not have the liberty to just speak loosely about any servant of God at any time.

When Saul saw that the armies were going to conquer him, he fell on his sword and committed suicide, but he did not die. A young man, the son of an Amalekite, was passing by and Saul asked him to kill him (Saul). So he went and completed the killing of Saul. He took Saul's bracelet and ran to David and told him he had killed David's worst enemy. He thought David was going to celebrate him. David realised that the young man thought nothing of killing the Lord's anointed. David asked him, *"Were you not afraid to put forth your hand to destroy the Lord's anointed?"*

2 Samuel 1:14-15
[14] So David said to him, "How was it you were not afraid to put forth your hand to destroy the LORD's anointed?" [15] Then David called one of the young men and said, "Go near, and execute him!" And he struck him so that he died.

Saul was persecuting David and he tried to destroy David. But David still honoured Saul, even though Saul was wrong. David instructed his man to kill the young man. Do you know that Saul was wrong? Maybe you know about a preacher who has done wrong and people are standing up against him. They feel he is not called by God for the wrong he has done. They speak any way they like against him because they feel he has done greatly wrong. I want to tell you, no matter what wrong the preacher may have committed, it does not give any person the right to dishonour him. Please read the full story in 1 Samuel 1.

If you do not agree with what I am saying, I want you to take a period of time and see how people's lives turn out when they dishonour preachers. You will notice families that were once prominent church attendees begin to fall apart and their children become hooked on the things of the world. I have personally seen talented families who should have been number one artists in the gospel music industry starting to struggle because they dishonoured servants of God. Don't dishonour God's anointed ones, no matter what wrong they may have committed, then the curse of the Prophets shall not come upon your household.

Cursed because they discussed Moses

Numbers 12:8
[8] I speak with him face to face, Even plainly, and not in dark sayings; And he sees the form of the LORD. Why then were you not afraid to speak against My servant Moses?

Miriam and Aaron discussed Moses in a negative light. They dishonoured him. He was wrong. But God came down and cursed them. God told them, *"I speak to him face to face."* God was telling them, "If there is anything to correct, I will correct him." God asked them the same question that David asked the nameless son of the Amalekite, *"Were you not afraid to speak against Moses?"*

Cursed for going against the word of David

2 Samuel 3:28-29
[28] Afterward, when David heard it, he said, "My kingdom and I are guiltless before the LORD forever of the blood of Abner the son of Ner. [29] Let it rest on the head of Joab and on all his father's house; and let there never fail to be in the house of Joab one who has a discharge or is a leper, who leans on a staff or falls by the sword, or who lacks bread."

David cursed Joab for having gone against his word. I want you to notice that this curse was placed on his entire family.

Cursed for despising the Prophet's judgement

2 Kings 5:27
[27] Therefore the leprosy of Naaman shall cling to you and your descendants forever. And he went out from his presence leprous, as hite as snow.

Gehazi, the servant of the Prophet Elisha, did not agree with the judgement of Elisha when Elisha refused to take gifts from Naaman. Elisha had already seen in the Spirit that Naaman had dishonoured him. Gehazi was not happy with how Elisha handled the case and he went after Naaman and took some of the gifts. By so doing he brought a curse upon him and his entire family.

You might be in a church and serving in the house of God. Maybe you are a deacon, an elder, a steward, an usher, a musician, an assistant Pastor or a church worker and you do not agree with a certain decision your Pastor has made. Be careful, he is called by God. You don't know why he decided what he decided and even if you think you know, don't judge his decisions. Don't go behind his back and make people negative about him. Don't spread stories and have discussions about your Leader; you are bringing curses upon yourself. You have not been appointed as a leader to control or judge the decisions of your Pastor. God called him, not you.

Cursd for exposing his father's nakedness

Noah made wine and he was drunk. One of his sons, Ham, found his father and went to tell his brothers. He saw his father's nakedness and he felt he could tell it to them. He felt he had the right to expose the wrong of his father. Ham was cursed and that curse affected his generations.

This situation still repeats itself in the world today. Many children rise up against their fathers because they feel their fathers did not father them well. Others rise up against spiritual leaders and feel it is their job to expose whatever they think is something wicked. There is a curse in such behaviour. Noah was drunk, but God still saw him as a father. The son who covered his father's nakedness was blessed. The one who exposed it was cursed.

People who persecute preachers are thinking they do God and Christianity a favour

Most people who persecute preachers and feel a righteous need to expose the wrongdoings of preachers think they are doing God a huge favour. It was so in the days of Jesus. Those who crucified Jesus believed that they were protecting their faith. They felt that Jesus was not sent by God and that He was a false prophet. They wanted to protect many people from being influenced by Him, so they crucified Him. Little did they know that He was indeed sent of God.

John 16:2 NKJV
[2] They will put you out of the synagogues; yes, the time is coming that whoever kills you will think that he offers God service.

I want to ask you a question. How do you know whether you would have been one of those who crucified Jesus or one of His faithful disciples? It is easy to tell. If you are one of those who have something negative to say about other preachers, calling them false prophets, you would have done the same with Jesus. There were many things in the ministry of Jesus that were against the normal status quo. Just because you don't understand a minister or you do not feel connected to his ministry does not mean he is false. Your spirit will not connect with every preacher, but that does not make them wrong or right. Flow with those whom your spirit connects with and leave judgement up to God. If God has not appointed you as the defender of His church, please don't appoint yourself.

How to break the curse of the prophet

I have taken my time and showed you different scenarios that can bring the curse of the Prophet into your life. Believe me, there are even more scenarios in the Bible. I just took a few. Now I want to show you how to break the curse of the Prophets.

Repent

If you have spoken in secret against a servant of God, repent before God. Ask God to forgive you your wrong. Repent and don't do it again. If you have had a confrontation with a servant of God and a curse was spoken over your life and you are still living in animosity with the servant of God, call him, send a message or go see him and ask him to forgive you. If for some reason you cannot get hold of the servant of God, just repent before God or go to another servant of God and ask them to pray with you to repent from the wrong you have done. After you have repented, don't be double-minded about it. Receive the Grace of God and move on with your life. If you have asked forgiveness and the other person ignored you or they were still bitter, be assured that God has forgiven you. Don't condemn yourself anymore.

Moses prayed for Miriam and Aaron when they repented

Numbers 12:11-13
[11] So Aaron said to Moses, "Oh, my lord! Please do not lay this sin on us, in which we have done foolishly and in which we have sinned. [12] Please do not let her be as one dead, whose flesh is half consumed when he comes out of his mother's womb!" [13] So Moses cried out to the LORD, saying, "Please heal her, O God, I pray!"

Bless the prophet

Instead of speaking against ministers of the gospel, rather bless them so a blessing can be upon you.

Genesis 12:3
[3] I will bless those who bless you, And I will curse him who curses you; And in you all the families of the earth shall be blessed.

Do not judge

If you do not understand the ways of a certain Prophet, don't judge. Leave judgement to God.

Receive the prophet as a prophet

Don't make fun of those who serve the Prophets of God. There is a Blessing for those who even give a cup of water to a Prophet.

Matthew 10:41-42

[41] He who receives a prophet in the name of a prophet shall receive a prophet's reward. And he who receives a righteous man in the name of a righteous man shall receive a righteous man's reward. [42] And whoever gives one of these little ones only a cup of cold water in the name of a disciple, assuredly, I say to you, he shall by no means lose his reward.

Honour the prophets

There is a blessing when you honour a Prophet of God.

2 Chronicles 20:20

[20] So they rose early in the morning and went out into the Wilderness of Tekoa; and as they went out, Jehoshaphat stood and said, "Hear me, O Judah and you inhabitants of Jerusalem: Believe in the LORD your God, and you shall be established; believe His prophets, and you shall prosper."

• A financial curse

To have a curse on your finances can be one of the most frustrating things in life. There is nothing more frustrating than earning a good salary or getting a big pay-out, but you can't prove what you have done with the money. There are people who do a little with a lot because of the curse, and there are others who do a lot with a little because of the blessing. I believe a financial curse is one of the easiest curses to break. God wants you to live in the blessing when it comes to finances. He does not want you to always be in debt and have unnecessary arguments in your household about finances. In the book of Malachi, God told us exactly how to break a financial curse and how to release the blessing of abundance. It is very easy. You may think you know exactly what Malachi 3 says, but I want you to take time now and read the following verses attentively:

Malachi 3:8-12

[8] "Will a man rob God? Yet you have robbed Me! But you say, 'In what way have we robbed You?' In tithes and offerings. [9] You are cursed with a curse, For you have robbed Me, Even this whole nation. [10] Bring all the tithes into the storehouse, That there may be food in My house, And try Me now in this," Says the LORD of hosts, "If I will not open for you the windows of heaven And pour out for you such blessing That there will not be room enough to receive it. [11] And I will rebuke the devourer for your sakes, So that he will not destroy the fruit of your ground, Nor shall the vine fail to bear fruit for you in the field," Says the LORD of hosts; [12] "And all nations will call you blessed, For you will be a delightful land," Says the LORD of hosts.

Did you know that some people just read this verse and close the Bible and nothing changes about their financial behaviour? They have found the key to their financial prosperity but they will not use it to unlock financial prosperity. By their actions they somehow think they can prosper just automatically.

Sometimes I feel so sorry when I minister on the prayer line and I read prayer cards that say, "Pray for me for financial prosperity" or, "I don't know what I do with my money; please pray for me." My heart goes out to such people. I would pray for them and deep within myself ask the Holy Spirit to guide them to the truth about financial abundance. You might wonder why I don't just tell them right there what to do. My question to you is, "How would you feel if you are going to a church for prayer and the Pastor just tells you to pay your tithes in front of all the people?" You might have a lot to say to your friends and family about this materialistic Pastor, won't you? When you become a member of a healthy church, and as long as you are hungry for God, the Holy Spirit will guide you and show you where the blockages are in some areas of your life.

Did you notice in the verse above that God says there is a curse on a person who does not give their tithe and offering? Do you really think a person with a financial curse in their life will do well financially? It is no surprise if a non-tither is struggling financially. It is biblical. Choose to break the financial curse on your life by becoming a faithful tither from this month. Give your tithes to the house of God where you fellowship and not as alms to the poor because you don't trust the Pastor.

• The curse of men

The curses of men are curses that are swung around by ordinary people. Such curses can be the result of anger, fear or jealousy. Some parents might curse their children out of anger. One person may curse another out of anger caused by an argument or disagreement.

Curses that are caused by fear are when your progress becomes fearful to someone who sees you as their enemy. When Balak saw the multitude of the Israelites, he called Balaam to come and curse them for him. This can happen many times in politics or the workplace when one man becomes too powerful for his colleagues so that they might feel threatened and try to block his way.

A curse of jealousy is when someone becomes jealous of the progress of another. Such a curse is caused by greed. If you progress too fast in the workplace your colleagues might become jealous of you and try anything in their power to block your way.

There are people in this life who would want to inflict curses upon you because of jealousy. But as a Christian, you have no need to worry and go through life fearing that people will be able to curse you. You should place your faith in the authority of the word of God and know you have the Blessing of Abraham upon your life. There are places where Christians are told not to even hug other people or to let them into their houses because those people can easily curse them or rub something on them that will block their Blessings. Christianity is not so weak that you have to walk around in fear because somebody might curse or bewitch you.

God has given you authority to bind things on earth and it will be bound in heaven. If you loose things on earth, they will be loosed in heaven. Use your authority. The Blessing of Abraham is upon your life and nobody can curse you. I want you to read the account of the Israelites when Balak called Balaam to curse them, because he had become envious of them. God turned every curse into a blessing in Balaam's mouth because the blessing of Abraham was upon the Israelites. That is what He will do for you. Don't walk in fear.

Numbers 22:1-3, 5-6 NKJV
[1] Then the children of Israel moved, and camped in the plains of Moab on the side of the Jordan across from Jericho. [2] Now Balak the son of Zippor saw all that Israel had done to the Amorites. [3] And Moab was exceedingly afraid of the people because they were many, and Moab was sick with dread because of the children of Israel. [5] Then he sent messengers to Balaam the son of Beor at Pethor, which is near the River in the land of the sons of his people, to call him, saying: "Look, a people has come from Egypt. See, they cover the face of the earth, and are settling next to me! [6] Therefore please come at once, curse this people for me, for they are too mighty for me. Perhaps I shall be able to defeat them and drive them out of the land, for I know that he whom you bless is blessed, and he whom you curse is cursed."

God will turn the curse into a blessing

Deuteronomy 23:5 NKJV
[5] Nevertheless the LORD your God would not listen to Balaam, but the LORD your God turned the curse into a blessing for you, because the LORD your God loves you.

Believe that God will turn every curse against your name into a blessing. Whoever tries to slander your name will turn and uplift it. God will close the ears of your boss to not listen to the bad news others are spreading about you.

I want you to be unreservedly certain that nobody will be able to curse you. Keep standing on the word of God and declare what the Word says. Take the following verses and stand upon them:

• No conspiracy shall stand against you

Isaiah 8:11-12 NKJV
[11] For the LORD spoke thus to me with a strong hand, and instructed me that I should not walk in the way of this people, saying: [12] "Do not say, 'A conspiracy,' Concerning all that this people call a conspiracy, Nor be afraid of their threats, nor be troubled."

From today I want you to believe and speak it over your life that no conspiracy shall stand against you. Don't fear what others fear in the workplace or in business. They may have false cases or accusations against you to try and work you out, to make your business fail or to taint your character, don't be afraid. Stand and see the salvation of the Lord. Don't give in to their threats. Very soon they will disappear like mist before the sun. You just stay in faith and keep speaking the Word. Stop saying, "People are conspiring against me." Start saying, "Their conspiracy shall not work."

• You will multiply in the workplace and in your business

Deuteronomy 30:9
[9] The LORD your God will make you abound in all the work of your hand, in the fruit of your body, in the increase of your livestock, and in the produce of your land for good. For the LORD will again rejoice over you for good as He rejoiced over your fathers.

Exodus 1:6-7 NKJV
[6] And Joseph died, all his brothers, and all that generation. [7] But the children of Israel were fruitful and increased abundantly,

multiplied and grew exceedingly mighty; and the land was filled with them.

Start believing that nobody can block your blessing. You will flourish in the workplace and in business against all the ill wishes of others.

• The righteous shall always rise

Proverbs 24:15-16 NKJV
[15] Do not lie in wait, O wicked man, against the dwelling of the righteous; Do not plunder his resting place; [16] For a righteous man may fall seven times And rise again, But the wicked shall fall by calamity.

Take some time right now in earnest prayer and see yourself rising. Speak the following declarations over your life:

- No conspiracy shall succeed against me.
- God is turning every curse into a blessing.
- Everything is working into my favour right now.
- I always win.
- I am rising higher and higher.

CHAPTER 10

JESUS IN A MODERN-DAY WORLD

We have a story to tell. The story of the crucifixion of Jesus is not based on a true story, it is a true story. To me it is the most beautiful story. Oh, it blesses me every time I tell it. You should never get tired of the story of Jesus. Never get to the point where you are saying, "I am tired of the same story every year." You don't know the full story yet. You should tell this story to your children, tell it to your family, tell it to your friends, tell it to your enemies, tell it to strangers, tell it to your colleagues and tell it to the world.

What is the story?

- God sent Jesus to die for the sins of the world.
- What was the reason why they crucified Jesus?
- What moved those who crucified Him to the point where they decided to crucify Him?
- What made them so angry with Jesus?

- Why did Jesus have to do it?

Jesus healed the paralytic who lay next to the pool of Bethesda and who had an infirmity for thirty-eight years. The healing took place on a Sabbath day, a day that was sacred to the Jews. They kept the law in every sense of the word. Jesus healing the paralytic on a Sabbath was to them a disregard of the Law of Moses and they wanted to kill Him for that. But then Jesus made a statement that moved them all the more to want to kill Him. He said He was the son of God.

The good deed that started it all

John 5:1-15 NKJV
[1] After this there was a feast of the Jews, and Jesus went up to Jerusalem. [2] Now there is in Jerusalem by the Sheep Gate a pool, which is called in Hebrew, Bethesda, having five porches. [3] In these lay a great multitude of sick people, blind, lame, paralyzed, waiting for the moving of the water. [4] For an angel went down at a certain time into the pool and stirred up the water; then whoever stepped in first, after the stirring of the water, was made well of whatever disease he had. [5] Now a certain man was there who had an infirmity thirty-eight years. [6] When Jesus saw him lying there, and knew that he already had been in that condition a long time, He said to him, "Do you want to be made well?" [7] The sick man answered Him, "Sir, I have no man to put me into the pool when the water is stirred up; but while I am coming, another steps down before me." [8] Jesus said to him, "Rise, take up your bed and walk." [9] And immediately the man was made well, took up his bed, and walked. And that day was the Sabbath. [10] The Jews therefore said to him who was cured, "It is the Sabbath; it is not lawful for you to carry your bed." [11] He answered them, "He who made me well said to me, 'Take up your bed and walk.'" [12] Then they asked him, "Who is the Man who said to you, 'Take up your bed and walk'?" [13] But the one who was healed did not know who it was, for Jesus had withdrawn, a multitude being in that place. [14] Afterward Jesus found him in the temple, and said to him, "See, you have been made

well. Sin no more, lest a worse thing come upon you." [15] The man departed and told the Jews that it was Jesus who had made him well.

You would have thought that when they saw the paralytic healed, they would have rejoiced over his healing more than being worried about the keeping of the Sabbath. The Law gave them hearts of stone, so they had no feelings of compassion for their neighbour.

They sought to kill Him

John 5:16-18 NKJV
[16] For this reason the Jews persecuted Jesus, and sought to kill Him, because He had done these things on the Sabbath. [17] But Jesus answered them, "My Father has been working until now, and I have been working." [18] Therefore the Jews sought all the more to kill Him, because He not only broke the Sabbath, but also said that God was His Father, making Himself equal with God.

He said He was the son of God

The very fact that Jesus said He was the son of God was the reason why people wanted to crucify Him. All His life Jesus had to fight for His identity. He was denied of being whom He said He was, the son of God. He was crucified for that very statement. People did not believe He was the son of God. You have to fight for your identity. Keep saying what the word of God says you are. If they say you are sick, keep saying, "I am healed."

His birth was questionable

The angel of the Lord announced to Mary that she will become pregnant and give birth to a child. She was shocked and told the angel she does not know a man. The angel told her that the pregnancy was of the Holy Spirit and the father of the child is God, and He will be called the son of God. Jesus was not adopted by God. He was born as the son of God.

Luke 1:31-32
[31] You will be with child and give birth to a son, and you are to give him the name Jesus. [32] He will be great and will be called the Son of the Most High. The Lord God will give him the throne of his father David.

Mary was impregnated by the Holy Spirit. Joseph, her fiancé, did not believe it; he was suspecting another man until God had to send an angel to him and claim the fatherhood of Jesus. It was only then that Joseph had peace with the fact that Mary was not pregnant with the child of another man. If God did not send an angel, he might not have believed. I wonder if he would have believed a Prophet?

Matthew 1:20
But after he had considered this, an angel of the Lord appeared to him in a dream and said, "Joseph son of David, do not be afraid to take Mary home as your wife, because what is conceived in her is from the Holy Spirit."

God confirmed Him at His baptism

At the baptism waters of John a voice spoke from heaven and said, *"This is My beloved Son, in whom I am well pleased"* **(Matthew 3:17).**

The Mount of Transfiguration

When Jesus was on the Mount of Transfiguration with Peter, James and John, God confirmed Him to be His son.

Matthew 17:5
While he was still speaking, a bright cloud enveloped them, and a voice from the cloud said, "This is my Son, whom I love; with him I am well pleased. Listen to him!"

God confirmed Him to Mary, to Joseph, to John the Baptist and to those present with him, and this time to the disciples who would be witnesses of Him. The devil also questioned His sonship.

The devil questioned Him

In **Mathew 4:3** the devil said to Jesus, "If you are the Son of God, tell these stones to become bread."

The devil was questioning Jesus on the authenticity of His sonship. He was questioning Jesus' identity. The fight was about the identity of Jesus. Remember He did it with the first Adam in the garden. Now He was trying it with the second Adam in the desert. He thought that Jesus, the second Adam, would be weaker in the desert. The devil will also try and question your identity in Christ. You got to keep standing on the word of God and say what the Word says about you.

Who do men say I am?

As Jesus was walking with His disciples He wanted to know if they knew who He was. "When Jesus came to the region of Caesarea Philippi, he asked his disciples, 'Who do people say the Son of Man is?'" **(Matthew 16:13).**

Jesus asked the question but He was not interested in what men said; He wanted to know what His men said. Peter answered the question under the influence of the Holy Spirit and said, "Thou art the Christ the son of the living God." That was the identity of Jesus. Peter knew who Jesus was. When Peter discovered Jesus, he discovered his own purpose. Jesus said to him, "You are Peter and upon this rock I will build my church." Peter's name means the rock. Peter preached the first message for the establishment of the church. His purpose was revealed when he pursued Jesus. Many people pursue their own purpose and they want to sprinkle a little bit of Jesus like luck dust over their purpose. Pursue Jesus, and He will reveal your purpose to you. You will be destined to succeed.

Jesus was not believed upon as the son of God. Throughout the life of Jesus, His identity as the son of God was questioned. The scribes and the Pharisees did not believe He was the son of God. The people of Nazareth labelled Him as the carpenter's son. They believed He was no better than His sisters whom they knew. Little did they know he was just sharing a mother with them and that God had to tell Joseph to accept Jesus because Mary was not pregnant from a human personality. Jesus' whole entry into the realm of the earth was unheard of. The question was how a lady could fall pregnant from the Holy Spirit. It has never happened before and it has never happened since the birth of Jesus. They thought saying God spoke to her was just Mary's way of escaping being stoned.

Are you the Christ, the Son of God?

Matthew 26:57,63 NKJV
[57] And those who had laid hold of Jesus led Him away to Caiaphas the high priest, where the scribes and the elders were assembled. [63] But Jesus kept silent. And the high priest answered and said to Him, "I put You under oath by the living God: Tell us if You are the Christ, the Son of God!"

Did you know that Jesus was crucified for saying that he was the Son of God? The scribes and the Pharisees did not believe He was the Son of God. They denied his identity.

The main reason why the scribes and Pharisees wanted to crucify Jesus was because He came doing all these wonderful miracles that convinced people to follow Him. Then He broke the laws of the Sabbath by healing people on the Sabbath. And He said He was the Son of God. They felt He was blaspheming God to say He was the Son of God. He was a major threat to their religion.

The son of a carpenter

The Jews felt that Jesus was just the son of a carpenter who had sisters and brothers whom they knew. He was making Himself equal to

God. Joseph accepted Jesus so well into his family that the public never questioned who His father was. I believe credit must be given to Joseph for accepting Jesus as his own son. He is a good example to many parents who have married into mixed families where they have to father or mother their spouse's children from another person. May the love and the interaction between you and your step-children be so genuine that the world cannot tell who your blood offspring are and who your adopted offspring are.

They did not want to crucify God; Jesus was the problem

Matthew 26:63-68 NKJV

[63] But Jesus kept silent. And the high priest answered and said to Him, "I put You under oath by the living God: Tell us if You are the Christ, the Son of God!" [64] Jesus said to him, "It is as you said. Nevertheless, I say to you, hereafter you will see the Son of Man sitting at the right hand of the Power, and coming on the clouds of heaven." [65] Then the high priest tore his clothes, saying, "He has spoken blasphemy! What further need do we have of witnesses? Look, now you have heard His blasphemy! [66] What do you think?" They answered and said, "He is deserving of death." [67] Then they spat in His face and beat Him; and others struck Him with the palms of their hands, [68] saying, "Prophesy to us, Christ! Who is the one who struck You?"

The scribes and Pharisees believed in God, but they did not believe in Jesus. Jesus was their problem. They loved God. They had no problem with God. Their problem was that Jesus said He was the Son of God and that He said He was the only way to God. For them the way to God was through the rituals of the Law. They had many commandments to keep in order to go to heaven. In their mind they were not crucifying God, though Jesus told them *"I and the father are one."* To them He was a mere man. That is the situation with many people in our day who disrespect preachers whom they think are not genuine. They see ministers of the gospel as mere men.

The world today still has a problem with Jesus

The world in which we live today also does not have a problem with us referring to God in general as just being God. They have a problem with us talking about Jesus.

For us as born again believers, everything changed at the cross. The cross of Jesus Christ is preaching to us. The cross of Christ is the turning point of our faith. Anybody can say they believe in God and in heaven, but Jesus Christ is the anchor of our faith. Everybody might believe in God, but not everybody believes in Jesus Christ as the Son of God. Jesus said, *"I am the way, the truth, and the life. No one comes to the Father except through Me"* **(John 14:6 NKJV).**

The crucifixion was about the identity of Jesus. The question was whether He really was who He said He was. Today we are facing the same challenge. The world is working hard to prove that Jesus is not the Son of God. Some believe that Jesus was just a normal man who happened to be a Prophet of God. That belief makes room for them to introduce their ways to God through other men. Everybody is claiming God as their saviour, but they dismiss Jesus, His Son. Jesus is still figuratively being crucified over and over again through their unbelief. They want to make no room for Jesus in a modern-day world. What they did not know is that Jesus does not need legislation, a physical temple or even a stable anymore. He lives with undeniable proof in the hearts of His followers. Our bodies have become the temple of the Holy Spirit and Christ dwells in us. They may limit our speech, destroy our material or even destroy our lives, but they will never destroy our beliefs. May you be steadfast and immovable like Jesus and keep finding innovative ways and methods to preach the truth without denying Jesus.

Insults on the cross

Matthew 27:39-44

[39] Those who passed by hurled insults at him, shaking their heads [40] and saying, "You who are going to destroy the temple and build it in three days, save yourself! Come down from the cross, if you are the Son of God!" [41] In the same way the chief priests, the teachers of the law and the elders mocked him. [42] "He saved others," they said, "but he can't save himself! He's the King of Israel! Let him come down now from the cross, and we will believe in him. [43] He trusts in God. Let God rescue him now if he wants him, for he said, 'I am the Son of God.'" [44] In the same way the robbers who were crucified with him also heaped insults on him.

They hurled insults at Jesus and challenged Him to do what they expected Him to do to prove His identity. There will always be those who think that Jesus does not exist because He did not prove Himself in the way they wanted Him to prove Himself to them. The proof to the things of the Spirit is given by Faith and not by doubtful demand.

You would have thought that after God had confirmed Jesus on so many occasions to so many crowds they would have believed Him to be the Son of God and spread the truth to others. Where have you ever heard of someone hearing a voice speaking from heaven, saying this is indeed My son? Even though He said He was the Son of God and broke their laws, was it not enough for them to believe Him for the works that He did? He raised Lazarus from the dead after four days. He multiplied five loaves and two fish. He opened blind eyes and healed paralysis. Was there really need for another sign? Amidst all the evidence they denied Jesus to be the Christ, the Son of God. They said, *"He said He was the Son of God."* I want you to know that they did not say He was the Son of God; they said, *"He said He was the Son of God."*

The unbelieving media and the persecutors of the church today also label Men of God, with undeniable proof that God is with them, as "self-proclaimed Prophets or Pastors." They feel if someone does not qualify according to their standards then he is self-proclaimed and therefore not called of God.

The moment of death

Matthew 27:46-53

[46] About the ninth hour Jesus cried out in a loud voice, "Eloi, Eloi, lama sabachthani?"--which means, "My God, my God, why have you forsaken me?" [47] When some of those standing there heard this, they said, "He's calling Elijah." [48] Immediately one of them ran and got a sponge. He filled it with wine vinegar, put it on a stick, and offered it to Jesus to drink. [49] The rest said, "Now leave him alone. Let's see if Elijah comes to save him." [50] And when Jesus had cried out again in a loud voice, he gave up his spirit. [51] At that moment the curtain of the temple was torn in two from top to bottom. The earth shook and the rocks split. [52] The tombs broke open and the bodies of many holy people who had died were raised to life. [53] They came out of the tombs, and after Jesus' resurrection they went into the holy city and appeared to many people.

Jesus finally died on the cross and His death was followed by strange occurrences. There was an earthquake, tombs opened, and dead people came and walked in the streets. They have been making fun of Him all along, but suddenly there was great fear upon them. They have crucified many criminals, but never has this happened. Never had there been any criminal who authorised his own death by his words. Never had there been an earthquake when a criminal died. What was this all about? Could he be the Son of God as He claimed? They were confused. At that point those who crucified Him acknowledged His identity.

Truly this was the son of God

Matthew 27:54
[54] When the centurion and those with him who were guarding Jesus saw the earthquake and all that had happened, they were terrified, and exclaimed, "Surely he was the Son of God!"

Finally the centurion who stood there came to the revealing realisation that truly He was the Son of God. He realised this was not an ordinary man. They denied Him to be the Christ, but at this moment they could no longer deny it. The evidence was too overwhelming.

You see there may be some who will deny Jesus to be the Christ. They will see Him as just a Prophet. But the Bible says that He has been given a name that is above every name and at the name of Jesus every knee shall bow and every tongue shall confess that Jesus Christ is Lord.

The centurion was bold in crucifying Jesus. He treated Jesus like a normal criminal. But he came to the point when he realised he had crucified the Son of God.

You and I have a story to tell. There are still many in this world who do not believe in Jesus. Everybody believes in God, but not all believe in Jesus. Those who crucified Jesus believed in God. They did not believe in Jesus. They did not believe that Jesus was the Son of God. They did not believe that Jesus was God. They saw Him as a mere Prophet.

We have a beautiful story to tell to our world. It is the story of Jesus. We live in a world where our message is under attack. We are subtly being forced to compromise our gospel. Jesus has become offensive to the world. Never give up on making disciples of all nations. Some will believe and change their ways, others will not believe, and others will persecute you. Rest assured that every knee shall bow and every tongue shall confess. Some will bow before He comes on the clouds, and others will bow too late when they see Him coming on the clouds. But bowing they will bow. Just do your part of spreading the good news.

The Antichrist

You may have heard about the coming of the Antichrist and you may have become numb to the failed claims of many who told you that certain statesmen were to be the Antichrist and their predictions proved to be untrue. I want you to read the following verse attentively and hear what the Apostle John is saying.

1 John 4:2-3
[2] This is how you can recognize the Spirit of God: Every spirit that acknowledges that Jesus Christ has come in the flesh is from God, [3] but every spirit that does not acknowledge Jesus is not from God. This is the spirit of the antichrist, which you have heard is coming and even now is already in the world.

We are living in the last days. Many Christians are waiting for a dramatic manifestation of the Antichrist. The Antichrist is already among us. Those who crucified Jesus were led by the spirit of the antichrist. They did not recognise Jesus as the Christ. The word *anti* means to be against something. In this context it means to be against Christ. The Apostle John said that the Antichrist was already in the world when he wrote his epistle, as we see above. So you should not wait for another, he is still among us. John also clearly describes the spirit of the antichrist. That spirit can be at work in any person just as a demonic spirit can be at work in any person.

If you read the scriptures I put forth to you correctly, you should by now be able to recognise the spirit of the antichrist in any person very easily. Every spirit that rejects Jesus as the Christ, the Son of God, is the spirit of the antichrist.

Do you know what is more shocking? Many Christians have fallen into the trap of cutting Jesus out of their success. They have packaged themselves to be accepted by the world. They become motivational speakers that are non-offensive. They cleverly push Jesus aside in their writings and in their talks. They use His principles but they deny using His name. They become acceptable to those who do not believe in Jesus. They do it all in the name of not being narrow-minded and reaching a broader audience for God. Their writings are filled with secular quotes instead of scriptural references. Many of them might be offended by my use of the scriptures to prove my points. I am a born again Christian writer who believes in Jesus, so I will use the scriptures. If it means that fewer people will buy my books, I am not moved. I have never seen the righteous forsaken nor their children begging for bread.

Jesus is the only way

Jesus is the way to God and He made it clear by saying that no one comes to the father but by Him. Take these scriptural references and stand upon it. Don't present your view, present the scripture. I don't have my own view. My view as a Christian is captured in the scriptures. The word of God is the handbook and the constitution for our Faith.

John 14:6 NKJV
[6] Jesus said to him, "I am the way, the truth, and the life. No one comes to the Father except through Me."

Salvation is in no other name

The Apostle Paul was clear in his day that salvation is in no other name but the name of Jesus. If we are taken to the court of law for saying salvation is only in the name of Jesus, it is not because of what we said or believe, but it is for what the Bible says. We are only saying what the Bible says.

Acts 4:12
[12] Salvation is found in no one else, for there is no other name under heaven given to men by which we must be saved.

This scripture has become a problem in our days. People don't want to believe that Jesus is the only way to God. The Apostles were stoned and some of them were thrown into jail, others were sentenced to death for preaching these words of Jesus. Our modern-day world is slowly but surely moving in that direction. Jesus Christ has become offensive to them.

Paul proved from the scriptures Jesus was the Christ

The Apostle Paul held public debates to prove to them that Jesus was the Son of God. The good thing is that they were willing to examine the scriptures and not some scientific reasoning of men.

Acts 9:20
[20] Saul spent several days with the disciples in Damascus. At once he began to preach in the synagogues that Jesus is the Son of God.

Acts 17:2-3
[2] As his custom was, Paul went into the synagogue, and on three Sabbath days he reasoned with them from the Scriptures, [3] explaining and proving that the Christ had to suffer and rise from the dead. "This Jesus I am proclaiming to you is the Christ," he said.

It has become needful for you and me to prove what we believe from the scriptures. You can't have a debate about Jesus from your views and opinions. You need to read the scriptures. Your answer is in the scriptures. The scriptures are not your words; they are the word of God. Respond to questions about your beliefs with scriptures. Your opinions do not matter. You did not write the Bible so you are not to be blamed for what is written in it. You are a Christian and you believe the Bible. So use the scriptures to communicate your convictions. You will notice that everything I have said so far was not my opinions. It is the scriptural convictions of the Christian Faith. Whatever I wrote was just explaining what the scriptures say.

Paul preached Jesus and Him crucified

The message of the crucified Christ is the message we preach.

1 Corinthians 2:2
[2] For I resolved to know nothing while I was with you except Jesus Christ and him crucified.

Jesus Christ is the determining factor of our gospel. The disciples were persecuted for preaching Jesus. The greatest message we must preach is Jesus. It is the message of salvation in Jesus' name; the message of healing in Jesus' name; the message of deliverance in Jesus' name; the message of grace through Jesus Christ; the message of faith in God through Jesus Christ. Can you see that it's all about Jesus? He is the way to God.

Many people think they can just take any road to God. They see Jesus as just another road. They reason it like one would just take any road to town. Jesus Himself said, *"I am the way the truth and the life no one comes to the father but by me."* Jesus is the way. There are no other ways. Not even Mary, His mother, is the way. The fight is about Jesus. Jesus was crucified because He said He was the son of God and the way to God. The disciples were persecuted because they preached Jesus. They are fighting us because they don't believe in Jesus, but they believe in God. The God they believe in is a general term. It does not refer to the God and father of our Lord Jesus Christ.

We have a message to preach

The world wants to blur the lines of truth and error. We must be convinced about our message. Our message is under attack. Are you going to stand like Shadrack, Meshack and Abednego or are you going to bow your knees to the gods of Pharaoh?

CHAPTER 11

HOW TO DEAL WITH THE STORMS OF LIFE

One time as I was preaching in a conference at a resort with a tin-roofed conference hall, a storm arose and it became difficult for the audience to hear me. I lifted my hand and commanded that storm to stop. As I lowered my hand, the storm subsided and died out eventually. The audience clapped their hands in amazement and it served as a great testimony of the power of God and the authority He has given us over the storms of life. God has given us the ability to control nature, if our faith allows it.

James 5:17
Elijah was a man with a nature like ours, and he prayed earnestly that it would not rain; and it did not rain on the land for three years and six months.

It means he was no different from us; if he could do it, we can do it.

I want you to know that figuratively speaking there are also storms in this life. You might face a storm in your finances, your family, your career, your business, or your marriage. There is a way you need to respond to those storms. God wants us to learn from the encounter Jesus and His disciples had with a natural storm. I want you to see how Jesus responded.

Mark 4:35-41

[35] On the same day, when evening had come, He said to them, "Let us cross over to the other side." [36] Now when they had left the multitude, they took Him along in the boat as He was. And other little boats were also with Him. [37] And a great windstorm arose, and the waves beat into the boat, so that it was already filling. [38] But He was in the stern, asleep on a pillow. And they awoke Him and said to Him, "Teacher, do You not care that we are perishing?"[39] Then He arose and rebuked the wind, and said to the sea, "Peace, be still!" And the wind ceased and there was a great calm. [40] But He said to them, "Why are you so fearful? How is it that you have no faith?" [41] And they feared exceedingly, and said to one another, "Who can this be, that even the wind and the sea obey Him?"

From this incident we can learn five very important lessons of how we should react to the storms of life.

What we learn from this incident

- Don't blame God for the storms.
- Get Jesus in your boat.
- Do not be fearful.
- Use your faith.
- Speak to your storm.

Don't blame God for the storm

I want you to note that instead of asking Jesus to calm the storm, the disciples started accusing Him of not caring. How can you accuse someone who was sleeping for something that happened while they were asleep? Can you imagine someone talking to you while you are asleep, then waking you up and saying, "You are not listening to me!" It is unfair, isn't it? The reason why they accused Jesus of not caring was because they reckoned there was no way that He could not have been aware of the storm. They thought He just ignored it for them to perish.

Sometimes people get angry with God because they think all manner of destruction that comes against them is God's doing or His permission. They will ask God questions like, "Where are you when things go wrong?" Some will ask, "God, why did you allow that to happen to me?" They have this belief that God is in total control of the earth and He just sits there and sees the devil attacking them and He does nothing.

Get Jesus in your boat

Mark 4:36
[36] Now when they had left the multitude, they took Him along in the boat as He was. And other little boats were also with Him.

If it was not for Jesus on this boat that day, the disciples were going to drown. This was going to be their dying day. Most of them were skilled fishermen who knew the stormy seas, but irrespective of all their experience, they feared for their lives. It means that this must have been a very fierce storm.

When you are facing challenges in this life you need to have Jesus in your boat to make it safely to the other side. Many people want to sprinkle Jesus like one sprinkles salt over an already well-cooked meal. They don't want Him totally involved in their lives. They just want Him to sort out their finances. They just want Him to open a door for a job. They don't want Him to tell them how to live. I want to say to you my friend that without Jesus your boat might sink sooner than you thought. You may be skilled and learned concerning the seas of life, like the disciples were skilled fishermen, but if Jesus is not in your boat your skill will fail you.

John 6:21
[21] Then they willingly received Him into the boat, and immediately the boat was at the land where they were going.

Have a willingness to receive Jesus into your boat. Stop waiting for a certain feeling or an appropriate time. Now is the time. You will reach your destination sooner than you can imagine with Jesus in your boat.

You know what is strange? I have heard hard-core sinners asking when things go wrong, "So where is God now? Why did He not protect this person?" How can you claim from an insurance where you are not covered? If Jesus is not in your boat, how can He protect you? If He is not forcing Himself onto you with salvation, should He now force Himself onto you with protection?

Do not be fearful

Mark 4:40
[40] But He said to them, "Why are you so fearful? How is it that you have no faith?"

The disciples were gripped with fear, yet they had Jesus in the boat with them. That is unfortunately the sad reality of the lives of so many Christians. They have Jesus in their boat, yet they are suffering all kinds of fears and anxieties in the storms of life. As a child of God, you have no reason to walk in fear.

Cast out the spirit of fear. We read in **2 Timothy 1:7** *"For God has not given us a spirit of fear, but of power and of love and of a sound mind."*

Fear is a demonic spirit and it is not from God. It is from satan. God will never use fear or fearful experiences to punish His children or to draw you closer to Him. God used His love through the death and resurrection of Jesus Christ to redeem us and to draw us closer to Him. As far as He is concerned, we are forgiven and provided for if we can only believe and receive it. The enemy will use the spirit of fear to intimidate and destroy you, but fear is never from God. You should always cast out fear with great confidence, knowing it's not from God.

Fear is an evil spirit. You have to cast it out with boldness. I want you to note that not only does the Apostle Paul say that God has not given us a spirit of fear, but he says God has given us a Spirit of Power. This confirms the words Jesus spoke to the disciples when He said, *"You shall receive power when the Holy Spirit comes upon you."* That power is the might of God. It is the power of The Holy Spirit. It is the same power with which Jesus performed miracles. It is at work in you right now.

Having a sound mind is a precious gift. As the world is moving toward curing the incurable physical diseases, we see mental illnesses on the rise. People are suffering from fear, anxiety, depression, schizophrenia, bipolar, depression, sleeplessness, madness and all other types of mental illnesses. It is easy to take a strong painkiller to deaden a physical pain, but mental illnesses are not easily cured by just a tablet. The power of God is the only invisible medicine that can cut through the soul and heal the innermost parts of the heart and mind.

When you face a storm, do not allow the spirit of fear to overpower you; no matter how overwhelming the waves may seem. Find your refuge in the presence of God. Do what you can to solve the matter but give the rest to God in prayer to do what you can't. Meditate on the Word and not on the threatening possibilities of the storm. Be aware that fear is anticipation of evil and it is baseless. Fear has no foundation to stand on. Eliminate your fear with faith.

Use your faith

Mark 4:40
[40] But He said to them, "Why are you so fearful? How is it that you have no faith?"

Jesus asked the disciples, *"How is it that you have no faith?"* He expected them to act differently in the storm. People of faith act differently than the world when they are facing challenges. You can chart your way out of sickness with the word of God. Build your faith through prayer, the scriptures, worship, fellowship with the Holy Spirit, praying in tongues and listening to faith-building teachings.

Speak to the storm

Mark 4:39 NKJV
[39] Then He arose and rebuked the wind, and said to the sea, "Peace, be still!" And the wind ceased and there was a great calm.

Jesus arose and spoke to the storm. He commanded the storm and the wind to cease and they obeyed Him. Jesus used His divine authority to control His circumstances. The disciples were panicking. They were worried and scared to death. Jesus, on the other hand, was calm and He spoke to the storm and controlled it with His words. On another occasion Jesus was walking on the sea. He took Peter for a lesson on walking on the stormy sea. Peter managed, but when he observed the waves, he started sinking. Jesus told Peter that he should not have doubted.

God wants you and me to use our spiritual authority and calm every storm we may face in this life. He does not want us to panic like the rest of the world. Take charge and rebuke the storms in your life. Speak to every challenge you are facing in your personal life, your family, your marriage, your workplace or your business and declare what you want to see happen. If you want to stay in the storm, then go around and tell everybody you are in a storm and it is very bad. If you want to stop the storm, then tell the storm to stop.

Did you notice that Jesus did not tell His disciples to hold on through the storm? He commanded the storm to stop. You don't need faith to hold on through a storm; you just need perseverance. But if you want to calm a storm, you are going to need faith. It is an error to tell people to hold on through the storm. It is unscriptural. You have to speak to the storm. We read in **Matthew 22:29** *"Jesus answered and said to them, 'You are mistaken, not knowing the Scriptures nor the power of God.'"*

There are messages going around that are in error concerning the storm. There are those who are teaching, hold on through the storm. You can't read the incidents of Jesus in the storm and come up with a theory of holding on through the storm. Your conclusion is in contradiction with the text. You have to speak to your storm. That is what Jesus did and that is the context of the text. The disciples were actually holding on for their lives and then they realised it was a very bad storm and something supernatural other than holding on needed to be done. That is why they got angry with Jesus. They knew He could do something supernaturally. According to Jesus' response He expected them to have done something. Jesus expected them to have had faith and not to hold on. He asked them, *"How is it that you have no faith?"* Faith was the key, not perseverance.

Problems with the hold-on-through-the-storm philosophy

- The conclusion is in contradiction with this scripture.
- The context of the scripture says Jesus calmed the storm. It does not say Jesus told them just to hold on until the storm passed.
- It eliminates faith. Anybody can hold on through a storm until it passes.
- It does not teach authority.
- It causes Christians to put up with the devil.

God wants you to be unaffected by the storms of life

Proverbs 10:25
[25] When the storm has swept by, the wicked are gone, but the righteous stand firm forever.

God wants you to stand strong when the storm is gone. You are going to need Faith to stand. God does not want you to suffer the same destructions as the wicked in the storms of life. I have seen many pictures of natural disasters where a church or a cross was untouched, with everything destroyed around it. That is how God wants to preserve you. You may face the same challenge an unbeliever is facing, but when it has passed, God wants you to shine brighter and be more outstanding amongst all the rubble around you. He wants to make you an outstanding showpiece of His goodness. He wants you to come out of the fire like the three Hebrew boys without the smell of smoke or a single hair on your body being burned. He wants you to reach your destination like a first-class passenger, well rested and fresh. Be bold and courageous and calm every storm right now.

CHAPTER 12

GET YOUR INHERITANCE

It's time to move from breakthrough to inheritance.

Acts 20:32
[32] So now, brethren, I commend you to God and to the word of His grace, which is able to build you up and give you an inheritance among all those who are sanctified.

The word of God is able to give you an inheritance. There is something to inherit. It is something you will not have to work for. It is a gift of Grace. As the Apostle Paul was planting churches and visiting them, he gave them something that will produce results in their lives in his absence. He knew he will wear himself out by trying to be god to the people, so he gave them the word of God. That approach has helped me greatly in ministry. I know when I give someone the word of God they will become strong, faithful and steadfast. Then I don't have to wear myself out by trying to control them with worldly wisdom. The word of God has an inheritance for you as a Christian. No human person can produce the joy and fulfilment God will produce in your life through His word. The Apostle Paul calls it *"the word of His grace."*

In this chapter I want to show you your inheritance in Christ and help you to lay hold of it. An inheritance is a free gift bestowed upon you by someone who died. Jesus died and there is an inheritance for you.

Hebrews 9:15-17 NIV
[15] For this reason Christ is the mediator of a new covenant, that those who are called may receive the promised eternal inheritance--now that he has died as a ransom to set them free from the sins committed under the first covenant. [16] In the case of a will, it is necessary to prove the death of the one who made it, [17] because a will is in force only when somebody has died; it never takes effect while the one who made it is living.

The will of God has been legalised through the death of Jesus Christ. Jesus is God manifested in the flesh. He died to legalise the will of God. As born again believers we have undeniable evidence that our testator died on the cross of Calvary. The will of God is now in force. We do not have to wait for Jesus to come again to give unto us healing, finances or deliverance. We can lay hold of our inheritance by faith.

Jesus died as a Testator to legalise the will of God. When He arose He was no longer the Testator, but He became the Mediator. Where there is a will there should be a legal mediator. A mediator is an advocate or lawyer that will enforce the wishes of the testator. Jesus is our legal representative. He has undeniable evidence in His hands of the death of the testator. The nailprints in His hands are proof. The wound in His side is the proof of the death of the testator. The empty tomb is proof. The many witnesses who confirmed that He was the same man who had been declared dead and who was buried, but is now alive, are undeniable proof.

You have an inheritance

All that God has, has become ours. We have become joint heirs with Jesus Christ who is the firstborn son. We have inherited the same power and authority. As He is, so are we in this world. I want to give you a list of what you have inherited from God through the death of Jesus Christ.

Salvation

*Are not all angels ministering spirits sent to serve those who will inherit salvation? (**Hebrews 1:14**)*

Power

*The self-same power that raised Jesus from the death is now at work in our mortal bodies. (**Romans 8:11**)*

Authority

*Whatever we bind on earth shall be bound in heaven. We have received the keys of the kingdom of heaven. (**Matthew 18:18**)*

Health

*By His stripes we were healed. Healing became ours at the death of Jesus Christ. (**1 Peter 2:24**)*

Peace

*The chastisement of our peace was upon Him. (**Isaiah 53:5**)*

Wealth

*He became poor that we might be rich. (**2 Corinthians 8:9**)*

Righteousness

*God made Him who knew no sin to be sin for us that we might be made the righteousness of God in Christ Jesus. (**2 Corinthians 5:21**)*

Land

*Every place we place our foot shall become our inheritance. The highest heavens belong to the Lord but He has given the earth to the sons of man. There is a piece of land for you in the earth. You have a goodly heritage. The lines have fallen for you in pleasant places. (**Joshua 1:3, Psalm 115:16, Psalm 16:6**)*

Victory

*No, in all these things we are more than conquerors through him who loved us. (**Romans 8:37**)*

What I want you to understand is that Jesus died for you on the cross and gave you power and authority over the work of the devil. He conquered the devil for you. He is the conqueror. You are more than a conqueror. You just step in and receive the victory. You don't have to fight the battle. You have to enforce your victory. This is where many Christians are struggling. They don't know how to enforce their victory. They are still waiting for God to give them victory. They do not see the cross of Jesus as sufficient for every battle they may face.

Obstacles to your inheritance

Any path to a destination may have obstacles that can delay or distract you from getting to your destiny. In the same way there are also obstacles that will cause a hindrance to your inheritance. There are three main obstacles that may block you from getting your inheritance:

- Childishness
- Ignorance

- Unbelief

➢ Childishness

Galatians 4:1-5

[1] What I am saying is that as long as the heir is a child, he is no different from a slave, although he owns the whole estate. [2] He is subject to guardians and trustees until the time set by his father. [3] So also, when we were children, we were in slavery under the basic principles of the world. [4] But when the time had fully come, God sent his Son, born of a woman, born under law, [5] to redeem those under law, that we might receive the full rights of sons.

The testator of a will normally sets an age whereby he determines the heir will have the necessary understanding how to manage his inheritance. A little child might give out money without understanding the value of the money. In the same way God gives His will to those who are of age. Those who are mature Christians are ready to handle the will of God. If you are a child in the faith you will not understand when others say they no longer get sick. It will sound foreign and unrealistic to you. You will think other Christians are naive when they say they can't get depressed, because on your level you don't see how a normal human being cannot be depressed or fearful. There are certain levels in the faith that you will grow up to. Until then you will be under the law, as the Apostle Paul says in Galatians.

Galatians 3:23-26

[23] But before faith came, we were kept under guard by the law, kept for the faith which would afterward be revealed. [24] Therefore the law was our tutor to bring us to Christ, that we might be justified by faith. [25] But after faith has come, we are no longer under a tutor. [26] For you are all sons of God through faith in Christ Jesus.

In the same way, when a child is not yet ready to handle the will, he is governed by the stipulations of the law. A guardian is appointed to manage the estate for his benefit. To some Christians who are not mature yet, that guardian is the law. Those who are mature are under the Grace of God. They have the keys to the Kingdom of heaven. They can open and close doors at will. Life is no longer a mystery for them. You mature in spiritual things through the right teaching and by faith. And all teachers and teachings are the same. Some teachings just identify with your struggles and make you feel like you are not alone, or you are facing something that is common to human beings. Some teachings build your faith to trust God for impossible things. Some teachings build your faith for finances and prosperity. Some teachings will limit your faith and make you depend on a worldly system. At the end of the day you become what your teacher is teaching. The day you have chosen your teacher of the Word you have determined many things in your life. Jesus said, *"A disciple is not above his teacher, but everyone who is perfectly trained will be like his teacher."* (Luke 6:40)

If your teacher is against prosperity, you will live in poverty. If your teacher preaches healing, you will live in divine health. If your teacher preaches on leadership, you will be a good leader. What are you learning from your teacher of the Word?

➤ Ignorance

God Himself said in **Hosea 4:6**, *"My people are destroyed from lack of knowledge."* This is the state of most Christians. Christ has freely given us health, salvation, righteousness, deliverance, favour, prosperity and eternal life as an inheritance through the death of Jesus Christ, but many Christians are still suffering and trying to achieve something God has freely given them. Many are looking for breakthrough instead of reaching for their inheritance in Christ. When you have your inheritance, a breakthrough will become irrelevant. Looking for a breakthrough, whereas God has given you an inheritance, is a manifestation of a lack of knowledge toward the scriptures.

The brother of the prodigal son did not know that everything his father had was his. He was working for his father's approval and for an inheritance. His father told him, *"All I have is yours."* All God has is yours.

➤ Unbelief

An inheritance is a free gift for which you do not have to work. You claim an inheritance, you don't pay for it. You have to believe that God has given you all things that pertain to life and Godliness. Your unbelief will cost you greatly. The Israelites could not enter into the rest of God because of their unbelief. They wanted to do their lawful works so God could provide for them.

Hebrews 4:2
For indeed the gospel was preached to us as well as to them; but the word which they heard did not profit them, not being mixed with faith in those who heard it.

See, you've got to believe to inherit what God has for you. There are saints that have gone before us and they have received their inheritance in Christ. If you don't have examples around you, the Bible is full of good examples such as Abraham, Isaac, Jacob, Joshua and many more. Read their life stories and imitate their faith.

Hebrews 6:12
[12] that you do not become sluggish, but imitate those who through faith and patience inherit the promises.

Stop chasing a breakthrough; take your inheritance

Over the years, people have built doctrines, conferences and series of messages around the breakthrough. I don't have a problem with it. I think there are people who need a breakthrough. What I have also learned is that once you have discovered your inheritance you will not run for a breakthrough, because there will be no need for it. Faith calls things that are not as though they were. Breakthrough is in contradiction with faith. Those who strongly believe in the doctrine of breakthrough will always defend their stance by saying, "I live in a real world will real problems." As if those who believe in the finished works of the cross are ignorant and unrealistic. The gospel of Jesus Christ and what He has purchased for us are as realistic as can be. We have an inheritance in Christ and we don't have to chase for little breakthroughs like slaves who receive small tips from their master.

What is breakthrough?

A breakthrough means to make a sudden discovery; to have sudden victory; to finally get through. Breakthrough means you do not yet have the victory but a time is coming when it will suddenly come.

The word *breakthrough* in Scripture

2 Samuel 5:20 NKJV
[20] So David went to Baal Perazim, and David defeated them there; and he said, "The LORD has broken through my enemies before me, like a breakthrough of water." Therefore he called the name of that place Baal Perazim.

The word *breakthrough* only appears once in scripture in the Old Testament. It is important to notice that in this verse, David fought the battle. He did not wait for God to magically intervene. He fought the battle and prevailed. He realised that it was just by the strength of the grace of God that he won.

Breakthrough is in contradiction with Scripture

The way people see breakthrough in our day is not in the same way it is depicted in the only scripture that talks about it in the Bible. David has fought the battle and he defeated the enemy. When he was victorious he said the Lord broke through. Many people are facing challenges and they expect the Lord to somehow break through and give them victory. Others are waiting for a sudden financial breakthrough out of their poverty.

This term was adopted by the modern church as something which God causes. It is seen as God giving breakthrough for you. Many people would say, "I am waiting for my breakthrough." Most of them actually mean, "I am waiting for the time when God will suddenly step into my situation and change it or cause me to win." That sounds all good and fine. But think about it for a while. Do you think God is standing and watching you fight a battle from a distance and then at a certain point he decides to step in and help you? Or do you think God is there with you from the start, waiting for you to command His power and bring an end to the work of the devil?

Breakthrough is in contradiction with the cross

Jesus became poor that we might be rich. He did not say that we might become rich. He said we are made rich. Breakthrough suggests a process of becoming. According to the finished work of the cross, God has already made us rich. He has already broken through poverty. There is no breakthrough we should be waiting for. We should lay hold by faith of what He has done for us.

We have become the righteousness of God in Christ through the death of Jesus Christ. God made us the righteousness of God. The word *made* is the Greek word *ginomai*. It refers to a state of being, and not a process of becoming. Breakthrough refers to a process of becoming. A process of becoming in the Greek means *metamorphosis*. The finished works of the cross are not achieved through metamorphosis (a process of becoming), but by *ginomai* (a state of being). Therefore you are rich and you are righteous. You are not striving toward righteousness or waiting for a financial breakthrough. The sooner you believe it the sooner God can release divine ideas, instructions and opportunities for you to locate your wealth and be righteous.

Breakthrough contradicts 1 Peter 2:24

[24] who Himself bore our sins in His own body on the tree, that we, having died to sins, might live for righteousness--by whose stripes you were healed.

Healing is not an area where a Christian should expect a breakthrough. According to this scripture healing is not a process of becoming (*metamorphosis*), but a state of being (*ginomai*). God is not going to heal you. He healed you. The Apostle Peter says, *"You were healed."* It is finished. It is done.

Breakthrough contradicts faith

Breakthrough says you are struggling until you get the victory. **Mark 11:24** says: *"Therefore I say to you, whatever things you ask when you pray, believe that you receive them, and you will have them."* You got to believe you have it before you can actually see it, touch it or taste it. The minute you say you are waiting for a breakthrough in any area of your life, you are cancelling the principle Jesus is teaching in Mark 11:24.

The idea of breakthrough is also in contradiction with **Romans 4:17** that says: "(as it is written, 'I have made you a father of many nations') in the presence of Him whom he believed--God, who gives life to the dead and calls those things which do not exist as though they did."

Faith calls things that do not exist as though they do exist. Breakthrough says you are still looking to become victorious in that area.

Inherit through faith and patience

May you start moving in Faith and call things that are not as though they were. Instead of waiting for God to break through, use your faith and speak things into existence. God has already done everything so we can use faith and lay hold of what He has already given us.

CHAPTER 13

TITHING

Tithing is God's way of providing for His work on the earth, and blessing His people financially. We pay taxes to governments who are not always living up to their promises. God has never failed us and as His children tithing is one of the ways in which we prove our faith and appreciation to Him.

How much is a tithe?
A tithe is ten percent of all your income. For example, it is R1 from R10 and also R10 from R100.

Who must tithe?

Everybody who receives money into their hands can tithe. You don't need a job in order to have a tithe to give unto God. You give tithes from your income whether you are employed or unemployed. Therefore everybody will have an opportunity to give a tithe. You can give tithes from your income at work, from your business income, from your rental income and from any financial gift you receive. All of us have money coming through our hands one time or another. An unemployed person may not have a steady income, but from time to time he/she might receive a financial gift of any amount from others. God wants us to be faithful with a little so He can entrust us with much. There are people who underestimate the power of their tithe because they are unemployed or having a low-income job. As a result they never see increase because God gives increase to those who can be trusted with a little. Get into the habit of giving God your tithe, no matter how little it may be.

The origin of tithes

The first time we learn about the paying of tithes was in the life of Abraham. He paid tithes to the high priest called Melchizedek.

Genesis 14:18-20
[18] And Melchizedek king of Salem brought forth bread and wine: and he was the priest of the most high God. [19] And he blessed him, and said, Blessed be Abram of the most high God, possessor of heaven and earth: [20] And blessed be the most high God, which hath delivered thine enemies into thy hand. And he gave him tithes of all.

This is the first time that we read about a tithe in the Old Testament. Abraham was the first man to give a tithe. He is our forefather. We follow the example of Abraham our forefather. We have the Blessing of Abraham upon our lives. We follow in his steps.

Many Christians claim the Blessing of Abraham but they are still poor. The Blessing of Abraham came upon him as a result of his faith. Abraham is called the father of Faith because he did not withhold anything from God. He gave to God even his only son. Giving requires Faith. A person who does not have faith does not understand how you can take from your income that is already not enough for your expenses and give a tithe to God. They just find it hard to believe. Once they develop faith they start giving and start seeing the blessing in due time.

Tithes during the time of The Law

The children of Israel also had to pay tithes during the time of the Law. Tithes did not find its origin in the Law, but they also had to pay tithes. God told Moses that a tithe of everything belongs to Him. The Israelites were instructed to give their tithes unto God.

Leviticus 27:30-32
[30] A tithe of everything from the land, whether grain from the soil or fruit from the trees, belongs to the LORD; it is holy to the LORD. [31] If a man redeems any of his tithe, he must add a fifth of the value to it. [32] The entire tithe of the herd and flock-every tenth animal that passes under the shepherd's rod-will be holy to the LORD.

Is tithing Law or Grace?

Tithing was instituted during the time of Abraham and also continued during the time of the Law. To answer this question further, we first have to understand the following concepts: Old Testament, New Testament, Law, and Grace.

- **The Old Testament** consists of the books from Genesis to Malachi.
- **The New Testament** consists of the books from Matthew to Revelation.
- **The Law** is the Ten Commandments that are written in Exodus 20:3-17. There are also other bylaws that speak about which animals were unclean, which clothing pieces the Israelites were not supposed to wear together, and so on.
- **Grace** is the New Commandment of Love that is written in John 13:34-35.

The Law was given in the time of the Old Testament and the New Commandment was given in the time of the New Testament. We are now living in the time of the Grace of God. We are no longer under the Law.

So far we have seen that tithes were paid before the time of the Law by our forefather Abraham. We have also seen that the Law is captured in Exodus 20:3-17. The book of Malachi that speaks about the tithe is in the Old Testament, but not in the Law. That is where many people confuse the two. They confuse the Law with the Old Testament. They think the Law is the Old Testament. The Law was given in the times of the Old Testament, but the Law is not Old Testament and the Old Testament is not the Law.

The very people who reason that the Old Testament is the Law still claim certain scriptures from the Old Testament.

- They still claim **Psalm 91:11** that says, "For He shall give His angels charge over you, To keep you in all your ways."
- They still claim **Isaiah 53:5** that says, "But He was wounded for our transgressions, He was bruised for our iniquities; The chastisement for our peace was upon Him, And by His stripes we are healed."
- They still claim **Isaiah 54:17** that says, "No weapon formed against you shall prosper, And every tongue which rises against you in judgment You shall condemn. This is the heritage of the servants of the LORD, And their righteousness is from Me, Says the LORD."

They are confused. They want to cut out their giving to the gospel but they hold on to God's giving unto them. How confusing.

So in conclusion I am saying to you that tithing is not Law, but it is Old Testament and yes we still need to pay tithes. If you don't believe in the Old Testament, why do you still have the whole Bible? Why do you not just have a New Testament? And if you only have a New Testament you will have to cut out almost half of the New Testament because it quotes and explains the Old Testament. At the end of the day you will have to write your own Bible and create your own heaven and hell.

Do we still need to tithe?

Yes indeed, as Christians we still need to pay our tithes. First of all, tithing takes care of the expenses that are incurred in the preaching of the gospel. Secondly we are instructed as a people of God to pay our tithes. That instruction is found in **Malachi 3:10** *"Bring all the tithes into the storehouse, That there may be food in My house, And try Me now in this," Says the LORD of hosts, "If I will not open for you the windows of heaven And pour out for you such blessing That there will not be room enough to receive it."*

Why do some Christians say tithing is not necessary?

1. You will have to understand first of all that not all who say they are Christians are indeed Christians. Some are agents of satan in the church.

2. Some people got hurt in church and instead of finding healing for their wounds they started looking for what they believe are faults.

3. Satan is behind the attack on the tithe and he has placed some Christians as his secret agents to persecute the church and bring confusion and doubt.

4. Most governments are threatened by the church, just as Pharaoh was threatened by the multitude of the Israelites. They fear that the church can mobilise itself and take over the government and make laws that are in line with the scriptures. So they politely instigate the media to write lies about the church to destroy the credibility of the church. They will publish scandals about influential church leaders. Nobody is perfect so if you dig deep enough you might find some dirty clothing in a clean house. That's why we need God. They will publish lies. They will publish the lavish lifestyles of some Pastors to

discredit them so people can lose faith in the church. All these things are the strategy of satan.

5. Governments know very well that in order for any organisation or group of people to accomplish their objectives they need funding. No organisation can successfully operate without funding. Not even a non-profit organisation. If you cut or reduce funding you cripple the activities and the effectiveness of the organisation.

You may or may not have known that even political parties can't grow their support without a financial muscle. A good manifesto does not guarantee success for a political party. The successful communication of the content and intention of the manifesto can lead to success. It costs money to communicate that manifesto to as many desperate voters as possible. The more finances a political movement has, the more effective it can market, and the more votes it can canvas.

If you go back to the life stories of national or global terrorists you will see the same trend. When a government closes in on someone they believe to be a national or global terrorist, they start cutting off his funds. If he has money in the bank, they start freezing his accounts because they know he will not be able to do much. They do the same with politicians whom they believe are responsible for crimes against humanity. They will freeze their accounts and persecute them in the international criminal court. You will also see one country implementing sanctions against another country. They cut trade relations to stop the effectiveness of that country. When they cut their trade relations, those businesses in that country that exported and imported goods and services are negatively affected. They cannot trade with citizens of that country and as a result that country's income is decreased and their effectiveness crippled.

I am sharing these things with you that you don't take the subtle attack against the church lightly. I want you to realise it is a battle between light and darkness. Don't just publish or comment negatively on bad news about the church. If you are of the light, defend the light, don't snuff it out with your comments. I want you to consider the following scripture slowly and thoughtfully.

John 16:1-2 AMP

[1] I have told you all these things, so that you should not be offended (taken unawares and falter, or be caused to stumble and fall away). [I told you to keep you from being scandalized and repelled.] [2] They will put you out of (expel you from) the synagogues; but an hour is coming when whoever kills you will think and claim that he has offered service to God.

Is tithing mentioned in the New Testament?

Tithing is mentioned in the New Testament. In the verse below, the Apostle Paul is telling us again about our forefather Abraham who paid his tithes. If tithing was not necessary, he would not have spoken about it.

Hebrews 7:1-7

[1] This Melchizedek was king of Salem and priest of God Most High. He met Abraham returning from the defeat of the kings and blessed him, [2] and Abraham gave him a tenth of everything. First, his name means "king of righteousness"; then also, "king of Salem" means "king of peace." [3] Without father or mother, without genealogy, without beginning of days or end of life, like the Son of God he remains a priest forever. [4] Just think how great he was: Even the patriarch Abraham gave him a tenth of the plunder! [5] Now the law requires the descendants of Levi who become priests to collect a tenth from the people--that is, their brothers--even though their brothers are descended from Abraham. [6] This man, however, did not trace his descent from Levi, yet he collected a tenth from Abraham and blessed him who had the promises. [7] And without doubt the lesser person is blessed by the greater.

Melchizedek was a priest, not under the law, and he received tithes. So tithes were not only paid under the law.

The Corinthian church was in the habit of collecting money when the Apostle Paul was about to visit them. So he encouraged them to rather put aside a portion of their weekly income. Though he may not use the word *tithes* here, he is referring to an amount related to your income.

1 Corinthians 16:2

[2] On the first day of every week, each one of you should set aside a sum of money in keeping with his income, saving it up, so that when I come no collections will have to be made.

They were receiving wages on a weekly basis and some were doing business on a daily basis, therefore he instructed them to set an amount aside proportionate to their income.

The Apostle Paul also instructed the Corinthian Church to excel in the grace of giving. He called giving a grace. As you excel in your career and in your health because of the Blessing of God, may you also excel in the grace of giving.

2 Corinthians 8:6-7

[6] So we urged Titus, since he had earlier made a beginning, to bring also to completion this act of grace on your part. [7] But just as you excel in everything--in faith, in speech, in knowledge, in complete earnestness and in your love for us--see that you also excel in this grace of giving.

I think if you were still wondering if giving was law or grace you should be convinced by this scripture that Giving is indeed Grace.

What challenges cause us not to tithe?

Debts

Mostly Christians honestly want to pay their tithe. They understand that it is part of their worship, but many of them are entangled in debts and they are struggling to make ends meet.

Ignorance

When a person is ignorant concerning the tithe they can be easily misled by others who tell them that tithing is just being under the Law.

A lack of faith

Paying your tithes requires faith. When people do not have faith it becomes difficult for them to pay their tithes. They don't understand how they should add what they see as another expense to their budget. For that reason tithing requires faith.

A love for worldly possessions

Your love for worldly possessions will be one of the greatest obstacles to you paying your tithes. The devil might convince you to rather buy clothes, another car, or furniture instead of paying your tithes.

The media

The media continuously try to discredit the financial system of the church by showing the lifestyles of certain ministers of the gospel. They are trying to tell the multitudes out there who are struggling that those Pastors are just enriching themselves at the expense of the poor. By so doing they try to create doubt and distrust. Meanwhile the Pastor has to be a father, a doctor, a shepherd, a lawyer, an intercessor, a motivator and many other things in one package and he still earn less than a doctor or a lawyer.

Where is the tithe paid?

You have to pay your tithes at the place of worship where you receive the word of God.

Deuteronomy 12:5-8
[5] But you are to seek the place the LORD your God will choose from among all your tribes to put his Name there for his dwelling. To that place you must go; [6] there bring your burnt offerings and sacrifices, your tithes and special gifts, what you have vowed to give and your freewill offerings, and the firstborn of your herds and flocks. [7] There, in the presence of the LORD your God, you and your families shall eat and shall rejoice in everything you have put your hand to, because the LORD your God has blessed you. [8] You are not to do as we do here today, everyone as he sees fit.

Did you know it is not so easy to find a place of worship when you are looking for one? It is easy when you are born again in a church because that will automatically be your place of worship. The place where you receive the word of God is the place where you pay your tithes.

Purpose of the tithe

1. To bless you

When you give your tithes and offerings, a blessing is released over your household by the minister of the gospel. That Blessing will cause you to be prosperous and do a lot with a little.

Ezekiel 44:30
[30] The best of all the firstfruits and of all your special gifts will belong to the priests. You are to give them the first portion of your ground meal so that a blessing may rest on your household.

2. To break financial curses

A man or woman with a financial curse is like a fish that is trying to swim against the stream in a flooding river. According to God, a financial curse is broken through tithing and offering and not by prayer.

Malachi 3:8-9
[8] Will a man rob God? Yet you rob me. But you ask, "How do we rob you?" In tithes and offerings.
[9] You are under a curse-the whole nation of you-because you are robbing me.

I have personally experienced over the years that when you give your tithes and offerings you do not have to pray for financial breakthroughs. You become like a farmer who has planted a seed. He does not pray for a harvest, he prays for rain. So when you have given your tithes and offerings, you should water your seed with words of faith. Uproot any form of doubt and unbelief like a farmer uproots weeds.

3. So you can grow spiritually

When a preacher does not have to worry about provision in his household, he is free to give himself to prayer and to the study of the word of God. When your preacher grows spiritually, you grow spiritually. Jesus did say that no student can be greater than his teacher. A preacher who has to worry about provision in his household will have little to no time to devote himself to God. The preacher who has time to study the Word, pray, prepare himself and fast will also be more effective than the one who has to run around worried, trying to make ends meet.

2 Chronicles 31:4
[4] He ordered the people living in Jerusalem to give the portion due the priests and Levites so they could devote themselves to the Law of the LORD.

King Hezekiah ordered the people to give their tithes to the Lord so the priests can concentrate on the work of God. Remember that the disciples also appointed people to serve at the tables, so they could devote themselves to prayer and the word of God.

Acts 6:1-4
[1] In those days when the number of disciples was increasing, the Grecian Jews among them complained against the Hebraic Jews because their widows were being overlooked in the daily distribution of food. [2] So the Twelve gathered all the disciples together and said, "It would not be right for us to neglect the ministry of the word of God in order to wait on tables. [3] Brothers, choose seven men from among you who are known to be full of the Spirit and wisdom. We will turn this responsibility over to them [4] and will give our attention to prayer and the ministry of the word."

4. To run the house of God

The gospel is free but the means to preach the gospel are not free. Most people will not in the winter go to a church that is in the open under a tree. Others have church buildings but they stay away from church in winter because it is cold. The church building comes at a cost; the chairs you sit on in church come at a cost; the sound system you hear the preacher and the singer on comes at a cost; the musical instruments come at a cost; and the electricity to light up the room and turn on the instruments comes at a cost. Some musicians come at a cost. The church needs money to successfully perform its duties.

To build the church

God is not happy when you are concerned only with your house while His house is in ruins. It is not a beautiful sight when people with expensive cars and designer clothes come into a broken-down place of worship with second-hand shop sound systems, noisy cables and sellotaped microphones. God wants us to beatify His house so He can take pleasure in it. Yes, God is pleasured when you beatify His church.

Haggai 1:4,8 NKJV
[4] Is it time for you yourselves to dwell in your paneled houses, and this temple to lie in ruins? [8] Go up to the mountains and bring wood and build the temple, that I may take pleasure in it and be glorified, says the LORD.

Landlords and business owners do not give buildings and building material for free to the church. The church will need finances to buy a building and building material. As you go out to your workplace, see this scripture being fulfilled in your life.

To finance the vision

God gives to each minister of the gospel a vision of what He wants him to do in the earth. Many times that vision includes building or purchasing a building. God will then cause His people to prosper financially so they can fund the vision and build the church.

Deuteronomy 8:17-19
[17] You may say to yourself, "My power and the strength of my hands have produced this wealth for me." [18] But remember the LORD your God, for it is he who gives you the ability to produce wealth, and so confirms his covenant, which he swore to your forefathers, as it is today. [19] If you ever forget the LORD your God and follow other gods and worship and bow down to them, I testify against you today that you will surely be destroyed.

God gives His people the ability to get wealth in this world so that His plans may be established. The job or the business God has given you was for the purpose of funding His vision on the earth. God has trusted you enough to entrust you with finances; will you trust Him enough to entrust Him with your tithes and offerings? Become a kingdom financier and establish the kingdom covenant of God.

To provide for the preacher

It is the will of God that the ministers of the gospel live from what is offered on the altar.

1 Corinthians 9:14
[14] In the same way, the Lord has commanded that those who preach the gospel should receive their living from the gospel.

Your tithes make provision to also provide for the preacher who is ministering the Word to you and praying for you when you are facing difficult times. God has purposed it to be that way. Everybody knows and sometimes quotes the verse that says a man shall reap whatever he sows. The question is, "Do you know why the Apostle Paul spoke those words?" I want you to see why in the next verse.

Galatians 6:6-7 TLB
[6] Those who are taught the Word of God should help their teachers by paying them. [7] Don't be misled; remember that you can't ignore God and get away with it: a man will always reap just the kind of crop he sows!

The Apostle Paul told the church that as they receive instruction in the word of God they should also pay the one who is preaching to them. It is Biblical for the minister of the gospel to be paid from the tithes and offerings.

What happens when we don't pay our tithes?

When a church does not give tithes and offerings, the preacher cannot receive an income. This has resulted in most preachers having to abandon the work of God and go into secular jobs to provide for their families. This was the case when Nehemiah came to Jerusalem. He found that the people had not been giving their tithes and the storehouses had run empty.

Nehemiah 13:4-10
[4] Before this, Eliashib the priest had been put in charge of the storerooms of the house of our God. He was closely associated with Tobiah, [5] and he had provided him with a large room formerly used to store the grain offerings and incense and temple articles, and also the tithes of grain, new wine and oil prescribed for the Levites, singers and gatekeepers, as well as the contributions for the priests. [6] But while all this was going on, I was not in Jerusalem, for in the thirty-second year of Artaxerxes king of Babylon I had returned to the king. Some time later I asked his permission [7] and

came back to Jerusalem. Here I learned about the evil thing Eliashib had done in providing Tobiah a room in the courts of the house of God. [8] I was greatly displeased and threw all Tobiah's household goods out of the room. [9] I gave orders to purify the rooms, and then I put back into them the equipment of the house of God, with the grain offerings and the incense. [10] I also learned that the portions assigned to the Levites had not been given to them, and that all the Levites and singers responsible for the service had gone back to their own fields.

When the people stopped bringing their tithes, the storehouses ran empty, thus the priests and the Levites went out to the field to work and provide for their families. Eliashib the priest started renting out the empty storehouse to Tobiah to stay in. When Nehemiah came he condemned the situation and he threw Tobiah's household goods out of the storehouse. He instructed the people to bring their tithes so the priests and Levites could be provided for.

This situation still happens today. Many Pastors have turned the church into a business because the people do not pay their tithes and offerings. Some are exposing the church to pyramid schemes and networking marketing for incentives. Others are turning church buildings into dormitories to make money from lodging. There is nothing wrong with the church having a lodge or renting out accommodation, but if the spaces that were previously used for the Bible school, Sunday school or worship services are turned into accommodation for an income, then something is wrong. I personally know of a church that was made smaller and the rest of the building turned into offices and accommodation rooms. Instead of evangelising to fill the empty chairs, they made the building smaller and turned the rest into a business. Your tithes and offerings are important for the funding of the work of God.

The difference between tithes and offerings
Tithing is ten percent of your income and offering is any amount that you feel led by the spirit or in your heart to give. The tithing amount is predetermined. Offering can be any amount. The key in

giving an offering is to listen to the Holy Spirit. The Holy Spirit has instructed me many times to sow an amount that has been bigger than my tithes. Offering is also important to God. In Malachi He said the people robbed Him of tithes and offerings; not just tithes. Jesus also sat at the offering basket to see what everyone was putting in, and He commended the widow who gave her last few coins. God wants us to give good offerings and not just small change.

Benefits of tithing and offering

There are surely benefits for giving your tithes and offerings. Let's have a look at them.

Malachi 3:9-12 NKJV

[9] "You are under a curse-the whole nation of you-because you are robbing me. [10] Bring the whole tithe into the storehouse, that there may be food in my house. Test me in this," says the LORD Almighty, "and see if I will not throw open the floodgates of heaven and pour out so much blessing that you will not have room enough for it. [11] I will prevent pests from devouring your crops, and the vines in your fields will not cast their fruit," says the LORD Almighty. [12] "Then all the nations will call you blessed, for yours will be a delightful land," says the LORD Almighty.

1. You break the financial curse

I have said it twice before in this book, and I will say it again: a financial curse is like a fish that is trying to swim upstream in a flooding river. One day, as I was reading that a person who does not tithe is under a financial curse, I realised how bad a financial curse is. I also realised that many Christians read this verse and still turn around and do not give their tithes. When you give your tithes you break the curse. The Blessing will cause you to prosper in all you do.

170

2. God will open the windows of heaven for you

Many people want to walk under an open heaven. An open heaven causes you to live a life of heaven on earth. While others are expecting to have no lack or shortage in heaven, you will have no shortage on earth. Your tithes will open heaven for you.

3. You will have more than enough

When I was growing up in church there was a brother who would have a testimony almost every week of how God had taken him from poverty to abundance. He said that he once told the Lord that he's got more than enough and God should bless others also. You see, God wants you to live in abundance. God will fill your fridge until there is no more space left. He will fill your wallet until you can't close it. He will fill your wardrobe until the doors can't close. He will fill your bank account until you have more money than month. Many people are still hungry when their food is finished. God will provide you with food that you will have to discipline yourself with the quantity you consume. He wants to give you more than enough.

I take my granny to the shops every year on her birthday and then I tell her, "You can choose anything you want. It does not matter what the price is and whether it is food, furniture or clothes." She always tells me without thinking twice, "I need nothing." She told me the other day, "I don't need more clothes; I have four wardrobes full of quality clothes." God wants you to come to that place of fulfilment. He will give you more than enough.

4. God will cause your business or work to flourish

God promises to prevent the pest from devouring your crops and your fruit from just falling off the vine. There are people who are doing much in business but they see little return. That is when the vine casts the fruit. It means before the farmer can harvest his fruit from the tree it becomes rotten and falls to the ground.

When you give your tithes, God says He will see to it that the pestilence and unfruitfulness are kept far away from you. Everything you put your hand to will prosper. You will do well in the workplace. God will see to it.

5. Nations will call you blessed

Do you know what it means for nations to call you blessed? Let me explain it in this way. A few years ago I travelled with my wife through London and we had a sandwich and cooldrink at the airport, while we were waiting for our next flight. The cost of the two sandwiches and the cooldrinks was almost R350. In my own country I would have spent less than R100 for the same things. The value of our Rand was weak against other major currencies. At the time I was so furious with our politicians who had contributed much to the weakening of the Rand. They do not feel the punch of our weak economy because they travel on our tax money and not from their pockets.

When I discovered this verse from Malachi, I realised that my prosperity was not in the hands of a politician. I realised that God can cause me to prosper and that even when I visit other nations I will be blessed. Years later I took my family to Disney World and one day I paid R850 for a chicken and rolls that would have cost me about R100 in my country. I was sad to part with so much money for a meal, but I realised that God had provided for me abundantly through the sales of one of my books. God can bless you in such a way that you are not only blessed locally but also internationally. That is the Blessing that rests upon the tithe. As you give your tithes faithfully, expect to trade in international currencies soon. Expect to travel the world and pay for your expenses with a smile because of the Blessing.

CHAPTER 14

THE HOLY SPIRIT

The Holy Spirit is the most important person on the face of the earth. But He happens to be also the most neglected, the most rejected and the most ignored person on the earth. Many people live their Christian life without the Holy Spirit. Others who are aware of Him have little to no interaction with Him. Jesus told the disciples that the Holy Spirit is someone just like Him. Jesus described Him as a personality and not just as a power or an influence. To fully understand the Holy Spirit it will help us greatly to study His workings in the life of Jesus. I want you to follow me as we study the Holy Spirit in the life of Jesus, and see how we can work with Him.

Born of the Holy Spirit

Luke 1:34-35 NKJV
[34] Then Mary said to the angel, "How can this be, since I do not know a man?" [35] And the angel answered and said to her, "The Holy Spirit will come upon you, and the power of the Highest will overshadow you; therefore, also, that Holy One who is to be born will be called the Son of God.

Mary was impregnated by the Holy Spirit. The Holy Spirit came upon her and she became pregnant with the Christ child. Jesus was placed in the womb of Mary by the Holy Spirit. Just as Jesus was born of the Holy Spirit, so every believer must be born of the Holy Spirit. When you are born again, you receive the Holy Spirit, which is the indwelling Christ. It is the start of your Christian walk.

Baptized with the Holy Spirit

Luke 3:21-22 NKJV
[21] When all the people were baptized, it came to pass that Jesus also was baptized; and while He prayed, the heaven was opened. [22] And the Holy Spirit descended in bodily form like a dove upon Him, and a voice came from heaven which said, "You are My beloved Son; in You I am well pleased."

The Holy Spirit came upon Jesus at the waters of baptism. Jesus was born of the Spirit. He was conceived by Mary through the Holy Spirit. On the day of His baptism He was filled with the Holy Spirit. The saints in the book of Acts were baptised in the Holy Spirit on the day of Pentecost. Every Christian must be baptised in the Holy Spirit. The baptism of the Holy Spirit is also recognised by the speaking of tongues. You can't say you have the Holy Spirit but you cannot speak in tongues. You may have a measure of the Spirit which is dealt to everybody to help them discern, but the baptism of the Holy Spirit gives you the indwelling Christ with the evidence of speaking in tongues.

Filled with the Spirit

Luke 4:1 NKJV
[1] Then Jesus, being filled with the Holy Spirit, returned from the Jordan and was led by the Spirit into the wilderness.

After Jesus had received the baptism of the Spirit He was now full of the Spirit. He was filled. The Holy Spirit became His navigator. The

Holy Spirit ordered His steps. Jesus followed wherever the Holy Spirit led, even into the desert. I wonder how many people would have resisted the Holy Spirit leading them into the desert. That might be the place where many would say, "Holy Spirit, I know my way home from here." Some would say, "I don't think this is the voice of God any longer." Jesus knew the voice of the Holy Spirit and He followed the Holy Spirit everywhere He led. There might come a time in your life when the Holy Spirit will lead you into a job, into a business, into a ministry, into an area where there are no luxuries to spread the gospel. Will you still believe the Holy Spirit has sent you when He sends you to evangelise the poor? Get to know His voice through fellowship, prayer and the Word, so when He gives you an instruction you will not hesitate to follow.

Tempted in the desert

Jesus was tempted of the devil in the desert. He withstood the devil with the word of God. In fact, the devil also fought Him with the word of God. It is one thing to quote scripture; it is another to quote the scripture as the truth. The devil was quoting scripture to cause Jesus to sin. Jesus refused to use the scripture to do what the devil said. Many people use the word of God to cover their sin. Some would use the word of God to cover their unrighteous living. Others would use the word of God to cover their drinking. They simply use the word of God to do what the devil says. Satan wanted Jesus to do so, but Jesus refused him. Jesus refused to use the word of God to please the devil. Use the word of God to do righteous works and not to justify sinful acts.

It was in the desert where Jesus had to face temptation. We read in **Hebrews 4:15 NKJV** "For we do not have a High Priest who cannot sympathize with our weaknesses, but was in all points tempted as we are, yet without sin."

Jesus faced the same temptation we face. As a believer, and especially as a minister of the gospel, you are going to have to face and conquer temptation to come back in the power of the Spirit. Great spiritual power requires a higher level of Christianity. You can't function on a high spiritual level with normal, mediocre and compromising Christianity. There is a level of power where much is required. You will have to pass the temptations and tests in the desert. The desert is the place where you are really vulnerable to what you are tempted with. Jesus was hungry after forty days. He really had the power to turn stones into bread. But He withstood the devil.

Jesus came to redeem the kingdom of God by His death on the cross. Here the devil was offering it to Him for much less effort. The devil was really making a good deal with Jesus. Jesus still refused and conquered. You have to learn to stand up in the midst of temptation and refuse what you are most vulnerable to, for the sake of the call and the love of God.

Jesus returned in the power of the Spirit

Luke 4:14 NKJV
[14] Then Jesus returned in the power of the Spirit to Galilee, and news of Him went out through all the surrounding region.

After Jesus withstood the temptation in the desert, He came back in the power of the Spirit. He went into the desert filled with the Spirit, and He came back in the power of the Spirit. It is possible to be filled with the Spirit and not have power. When a person receives the baptism of the Holy Spirit, they are filled with the Spirit. Many have received this infilling, but not many have the power of the Spirit. Many Spirit-filled, tongue-talking Christians are still being oppressed by the devil. They are still suffering oppression, discouragement, depression, sickness and despair. They have the Spirit but no power. To have power is to have authority over the devil and his works. **Luke 10:19** says, *"Behold, I give you the authority to trample on serpents and scorpions, and over all the power of the enemy, and nothing shall by any means hurt you."*

A believer with the power of the Spirit has power and authority over the works of the devil. Every minister of the gospel must be led by the Spirit into the desert where he will withstand temptation and conquer and have an encounter with God. He must come back with the power of the Spirit. After such a minister comes back in the power of the Spirit, great things must happen. When Jesus came back in the power of the Spirit, His fame spread all over the towns and cities. The Holy Spirit was His advertising agent. The power spoke for itself and the multitudes came. As a minister of the gospel you need to overcome the desert. You need to withstand temptation. In whatever area you might have been most vulnerable in the past, you need to withstand the evil right there. Don't fall for any skirt. Don't give up the power. When the devil tempts you with money, sex, worldly possessions and positions, just think what you are about to lose. Stay faithful, stay focused because great power is coming your way. You have already come too far to turn around. Great power is coming your way.

If you are studying in school for a certificate, diploma or degree, there are going to be times when you are going to have to refuse yourself pleasure. You are going to have to miss some celebrations, miss some outings or miss some television shows. There is a price to be paid. It is the same way when it comes to the things of the Spirit. You can't stagnate any longer. Say no in the face of the toughest temptation. Refuse to fall for temptation even if every part of your body is screaming out for that temporary satisfaction. Your reward is much greater.

Jesus told the disciples to tarry in the city. He instructed them to go nowhere until they had the Holy Spirit. It was after they had the Holy Spirit that they became powerful witnesses of Christ. The Holy Spirit ordains the minister into the ministry. Many people give much credit to the ordination of men. And yes, it is important, but there is a greater ordination. It is when the Holy Spirit sets you apart for Ministry. That is an ordination of great power and authority. If you can withstand the devil in the desert, he and his demons will flee when you enter the city.

The work of the Holy Spirit

Once you have the power of the Holy Spirit there are definite things that you will do. After Jesus came up out of the desert He gave the reason why the Spirit of God was upon Him. This is what's got to happen to you also.

Luke 4:18-19 NKJV
[18] The Spirit of the LORD is upon Me, Because He has anointed Me To preach the gospel to the poor; He has sent Me to heal the broken-hearted, To proclaim liberty to the captives And recovery of sight to the blind, To set at liberty those who are oppressed; [19] To proclaim the acceptable year of the LORD.

Jesus went into the desert filled with the Holy Spirit; He came out with the power of the Spirit. Multitudes followed Him. In the above verses He explains the cause of the power. He tells us the Holy Spirit is doing these things. Here is what Holy Spirit did through Jesus, and He will do the same through you:

➢ You must preach the Gospel

You cannot preach without the Holy Spirit. It is a waste of time. Sermons without the Holy Spirit are full of man's knowledge, self-knowledge, worldly wisdom, philosophy and carnal reasoning. Our word should be filled with the Holy Spirit. A sermon without the Holy Spirit is dry and tasteless. Sermons without the Holy Spirit will make the preacher uncertain, empty and depressed.

➢ Heal the sick

The minister that is filled with the Spirit must bring healing. He must bring healing to the spirit, soul and body of his hearers. Cancers will flee, headaches will flee, depression will flee, poverty will flee and whatever is of the devil will flee before you.

➤ Liberate the captives

Liberty to the captives refers to salvation, deliverance and the destruction of bondages. Bondages can be demonic oppression or false beliefs. When a minister has the power of the Spirit he can deliver the people of God.

➤ Give sight to the blind

This speaks of the miracle-working power of God. Giving sight to the blind refers to miraculous healing of the body. It includes lameness, deafness, the cripple and the mute. It also refers to all diseases of the body. This is what the power of the Holy Spirit will do: blinded eyes will see, cripples will walk, deaf will hear, mute will speak and the wheelchair-bound will go free.

➤ Free the oppressed

Oppression speaks of the diseases of the soul. It includes, depression, worry, fear, anxiety, madness and bipolar. A minister under the power of the Holy Spirit can set such people free. Thank you Lord, I can do it. Yes you can. The Holy Spirit has the cure for the diseases of the soul.

➤ The acceptable year of the Lord

In the ancient times, people had to wait fifty years for the year of jubilee. Under the power of the Holy Spirit, the minister can make a declaration and it will be so. Remember, Elijah spoke drought and rain into being. God is waiting to fulfil the predictions of His servants. When a minister that is full of the Spirit speaks, God fulfils his words. The minister can thus decide and declare the favour of the Lord at any time over anybody and it shall be so. He becomes a custodian of the favour, the blessing, healing, deliverance and the grace of God. Speak favour, blessings, healing, deliverance, promotion, increase and love over yourself.

Pastor Gerald Hugo

One goes the other comes

John 16:7
[7] Nevertheless I tell you the truth. It is to your advantage that I go away; for if I do not go away, the Helper will not come to you; but if I depart, I will send Him to you.

The words of Jesus in this verse are the most precious words concerning the Holy Spirit. Jesus told the disciples that if He does not go, the Holy Spirit cannot come. Jesus describes the Holy Spirit as a personality with personal attributes. Jesus does not refer to Him as a power or just and influence. Jesus refers to The Holy Spirit as a person.

Many people would have loved to live in the times when Jesus was still on the earth. Can you imagine having Jesus, the miracle worker, readily available at any time, how would that be? Did you know that Jesus is actually still in the earth just as He was back then? This time He does not have a physical body, but He lives in physical bodies. Jesus is now dwelling in you through the Holy Spirit. Jesus' body did not make Him God. His body made Him man. The Holy Spirit brought out the God in Him. If you have the Holy Spirit you are in the same position, with the same power as Jesus had. Jesus is yet again in the earth today through the Holy Spirit in you. I am not saying you are Jesus. Please don't get me wrong. I am saying Jesus is in you. We must come to the place where Paul was when he said, *"It's no longer I that live but Christ lives within me. If you believe that the same power of Jesus is now at work in you, you will do what Jesus did and the greater things He promised."*

Jesus came in the form of the Holy Spirit

John 14:16-20
[16] And I will pray the Father, and He will give you another Helper, that He may abide with you forever—[17] the Spirit of truth, whom the world cannot receive, because it neither sees Him nor knows Him; but you know Him, for He dwells with you and will be in you.

180

[18] I will not leave you orphans; I will come to you. [19] A little while longer and the world will see Me no more, but you will see Me. Because I live, you will live also. [20] At that day you will know that I am in My Father, and you in Me, and I in you.

Jesus promised not to leave us as orphans. He promised to come to us in the form of the Holy Spirit. Jesus and the Holy Spirit are one, just as Jesus and the Father are one. God physically came to the earth through the body of Jesus Christ into the body of one person called Mary. The second time He came to the earth in the form of the Holy Spirit into the bodies of many believers. It is so glorious. Hallelujah! God is in the earth again dwelling in the mortal body of the believer. This time He promises to stay with us until the end of time. When we walk in the consciousness of this reality we can do the same things and greater works as Jesus did.

The Holy Spirit represents Jesus

The Holy Spirit is the continued ministry of Jesus upon the earth. The ministry of Jesus still continues in the earth through the Holy Spirit. When the Holy Spirit CAME, He continued where Jesus had left off. He continues the ministry of Jesus in our bodies.

John 16:12-16
[12] "I still have many things to say to you, but you cannot bear them now. [13] However, when He, the Spirit of truth, has come, He will guide you into all truth; for He will not speak on His own authority, but whatever He hears He will speak; and He will tell you things to come. [14] He will glorify Me, for He will take of what is Mine and declare it to you. [15] All things that the Father has are Mine. Therefore I said that He will take of Mine and declare it to you. [16] A little while, and you will not see Me; and again a little while, and you will see Me, because I go to the Father.

The Holy Spirit is also the unlimited Ministry of Jesus. While Jesus was physically present on the earth, He was limited by space and time. He could only be at one place at the same time. Remember when He was on His way to pray for Jairus' daughter? He was held up by the woman with the issue of blood and Jairus' daughter died in the meantime. Jesus could not attend to both of them at the same time. On another occasion He was three days late to attend to the call of Lazarus' family. Lazarus was sick and he died. When Jesus arrived, Martha said to Him, "If you had been here my brother would not have died," signifying that Jesus' presence and the effect of His work were limited to space. Through the Holy Spirit Jesus is no longer limited to space and time. Jesus is now everywhere at the same time. The Holy Spirit can now be sent.

We need to note the following with great understanding. The Holy Spirit is no longer limited to one physical body as He was in the case of Jesus on the earth; He can now be present in whoever has welcomed Him. Secondly, the Holy Spirit is not limited to a physical presence. The Holy Spirit can be sent anywhere by whoever is filled with Him. Jesus had to be physically present in His days, before He dwelt in the earth by the Holy Spirit. Now He is no longer limited to a physical presence. The Holy Spirit now enables us to be in one city and minister healing to a person in another city. We can be on television and transfer the Holy Spirit through the television. You can read this book that I have written and the power of the Holy Spirit can come upon you as you read these Spirit-filled words.

The Holy Spirit promotes Jesus. If you are embracing the Holy Spirit, you are embracing Jesus. Some people get confused over whether they should mention the Holy Spirit or Jesus when they speak or pray. The Holy Spirit and Jesus are one. Jesus dwells among us in the form of the Holy Spirit.

Jesus said that when we receive the Holy Spirit, the world will not see Him but we will see Him. The Holy Spirit is Jesus in the earth again. Just as Jesus was present in the earth in days of old, He is still present through the Holy Spirit. He is just using different bodies. Those who still want to kill Jesus do not have only one person to crucify; they will now have to crucify Christians around the world. And the Holy Spirit is making His home daily in new believers as they are saved. They may kill some Christians in some countries but they will never be able to drown Christianity out, because of The Holy Spirit.

Jesus found His purpose in the Word

Luke 4:20-21 NKJV
[20] Then He closed the book, and gave it back to the attendant and sat down. And the eyes of all who were in the synagogue were fixed on Him. [21] And He began to say to them, "Today this Scripture is fulfilled in your hearing."

Jesus found His purpose in the word of God. That is where your purpose is. That is where you will find who you really are. Jesus did not look for His identity elsewhere. He found it in the word of God and He called it fulfilled. He saw Himself as the fulfilment of scripture and Bible prophecy.

Thank you Lord, I am the fulfilment of scripture and Bible prophecy. I fulfil the scriptures. You've got to say that about yourself. When you read in the Bible, *"These signs shall follow those who believe,"* you must say, *"This is written about me. Signs and wonders shall follow me."* You've got to find your purpose in the word of God. You've got to find your authority, your spiritual power, your healing, your salvation, your righteousness, your peace, your finances and your prosperity in the word of God. Once you have found it, you've got to believe and declare it. Say it until you see it.

You have power through the Holy Spirit

Luke 8:45-46 NKJV
[45] And Jesus said, "Who touched Me?" When all denied it, Peter and those with him said, "Master, the multitudes throng and press You, and You say, 'Who touched Me?'" [46] But Jesus said, "Somebody touched Me, for I perceived power going out from Me."

The woman with the issue of blood withdrew power from Jesus when she touched Him. Many people pressed on Him, but only one person touched Him. The Power which left Jesus' body was the power of the Holy Spirit. In fact, it was the Holy Spirit. Power is one of the attributes of the Holy Spirit. Jesus told the disciples they shall receive Power when the Holy Spirit is come upon them. The woman was thus healed by the Holy Spirit that was upon Jesus. The Holy Spirit was even on Jesus' garment. Paul also laid hands on handkerchiefs and the sick were healed through them. The Holy Spirit was thus transferred onto the materials. In this case the garment of Jesus was full of the Holy Spirit. The clothing of a minister of the Spirit is filled with the Holy Spirit. If you can also believe it, your clothes will be saturated with the Power of the Holy Spirit.

If you have received the infilling of the Holy Spirit with the evidence of speaking in tongues, I want you to know that you have the dynamic ability of Jesus Christ mightily at work in you. May you never feel defeated or powerless again. Charge yourself up with the Holy Spirit power through prayer and tongues.

CHAPTER 15

FORGIVENESS

Ephesians 4:32
[32] And be kind to one another, tenderhearted, forgiving one another, even as God in Christ forgave you.

God has forgiven us in Christ. All men are forgiven before God, but all men must receive forgiveness from God through salvation. There might be sins that are still in your conscious mind, but you were forgiven of them before God the day you pleaded for forgiveness. You might still be reminded of the sin by the consequences that still prevail, but you are forgiven in the sight of God.

The Apostle Paul is encouraging us to be kind-hearted and forgiving toward one another, just as Christ has forgiven us.

Forgiveness is the act or the process of setting someone free from a wrong they have committed against you. It means to choose to overlook a wrong someone has committed against you.

An eye-opening story about forgiveness

Matthew 18:21-35 NKJV

[21] Then Peter came to Him and said, "Lord, how often shall my brother sin against me, and I forgive him? Up to seven times?" [22] Jesus said to him, "I do not say to you, up to seven times, but up to seventy times seven. [23] Therefore the kingdom of heaven is like a certain king who wanted to settle accounts with his servants. [24] And when he had begun to settle accounts, one was brought to him who owed him ten thousand talents. [25] But as he was not able to pay, his master commanded that he be sold, with his wife and children and all that he had, and that payment be made. [26] The servant therefore fell down before him, saying, 'Master, have patience with me, and I will pay you all.' [27] Then the master of that servant was moved with compassion, released him, and forgave him the debt. [28] But that servant went out and found one of his fellow servants who owed him a hundred denarii; and he laid hands on him and took him by the throat, saying, 'Pay me what you owe!' [29] So his fellow servant fell down at his feet and begged him, saying, 'Have patience with me, and I will pay you all.' [30] And he would not, but went and threw him into prison till he should pay the debt. [31] So when his fellow servants saw what had been done, they were very grieved, and came and told their master all that had been done. [32] Then his master, after he had called him, said to him, 'You wicked servant! I forgave you all that debt because you begged me. [33] Should you not also have had compassion on your fellow servant, just as I had pity on you?' [34] And his master was angry, and delivered him to the torturers until he should pay all that was due to him. [35] So My heavenly Father also will do to you if each of you, from his heart, does not forgive his brother his trespasses."

You would have thought that this man would be more forgiving toward others after he had been forgiven so much. But it sometimes seems like people with the most skeletons always like to dig up the skeletons of others. He was supposed to be gracious after he had just received grace. It is always easy to point a finger at the wrong others may have committed when your wrongs have been graciously covered. God forgives us so that we can even forget what we have done wrong. That is good, but it becomes a problem when we become harsh and impatient toward others. When you become judgemental toward your brother's mistakes, God wants you to remember where He has brought you from.

This man was supposed to have compassion on the man who owed him and forgive him as he had been forgiven. Instead he became harsh and unforgiving.

The need to forgive

You would be naive to think you will go through this life and never be offended by any person.

They say in Spain there was a father and his son called Paco, a very common name in Spain, whose relationship was falling apart to the point where the son moved out and stayed on his own. The father did not know where his son was and he could not take it anymore, so he went to the newspaper and placed an ad. The ad read something like, "Paco my son, wherever you are, I want you to know I have forgiven you. Let's forget the past and move on. Let's meet tomorrow at 14h00 in front of the newspaper's office."

The next day the newspaper headline read, "A father calls on his son Paco to forgive him." And more than 800 Pacos showed up! Can you believe it? Everybody needs to forgive somebody. Nobody is perfect. So it's better to be aware that somewhere along your life you are going to have to forgive someone or ask for someone's forgiveness. That is life. Otherwise you have to go and stay alone on an island with just animals and your perfect self.

Forgive four hundred and ninety times a day

Did you notice that Jesus told Peter that we ought to forgive those who sin against us at least seventy times seven times in one day? Not seventy times seven times in your lifetime, but in a day. Seventy times seven equals the amount of four hundred and ninety. How would you feel if someone keeps on doing the same wrong against you four hundred and ninety times in one day? Or would you be one of those who would say after the second time, "This is enough; it is not the first time this person is doing it to me"? Make a decision to forgive those who have wronged you; not for their sake but for your sake.

Choose to be the better person

What might disappoint you the most in life is when you are being offended by someone you never thought would offend you. You might expect the other person to be the one who would initiate forgiveness and make things right, but if they don't, you can be the person to initiate forgiveness. Choose to be the better person.

No one can say they have never been forgiven. God has forgiven us of many sins. We need to forgive others of their sins against us. We read in **Colossians 3:12-13 NKJV** *"Therefore, as the elect of God, holy and beloved, put on tender mercies, kindness, humility, meekness, longsuffering; bearing with one another, and forgiving one another, if anyone has a complaint against another; even as Christ forgave you, so you also must do. Do not walk in unforgiveness it will cost you greatly."*

The cost of unforgiveness

The negative effects of unforgiveness

Forgiveness is the act or the process of setting someone free from a wrong they have committed against you. Unforgiveness is the unwillingness to set someone free from a wrong they have committed against you. Unforgiveness also means to hold a grudge against someone who has committed a wrong against you.

The cost of unforgiveness is too high. You cannot afford to walk in it. I want to list a few negative effects that unforgiveness will have on you. I call it the cost of unforgiveness.

➤ Unforgiving people go to hell

Matthew 6:14-15 NKJV
[14] For if you forgive men their trespasses, your heavenly Father will also forgive you. [15] But if you do not forgive men their trespasses, neither will your Father forgive your trespasses.

The irony is that most Christians think they can live in unforgiveness and go to heaven. I want you to pay attention to what this scripture says. If you do not forgive those who sin against you, your Heavenly Father will not forgive you. Where do you think people are going whose sins are not forgiven? Let me help you with the answer – they go to hell. Yes, they do. Can you imagine your whole Christianity being in vain because you walked in unforgiveness?

➤ You set the standard for your own judgement

Matthew 7:1-3
[1] Judge not, that you be not judged. [2] For with what judgment you judge, you will be judged; and with the measure you use, it will be measured back to you. [3] And why do you look at the speck in your brother's eye, but do not consider the plank in your own eye?

Many people judge themselves by their good intentions and they judge others by their actions. If they were to judge others by their good intentions, they will feel no need to condemn them. When you judge others, you set the standard at which God must judge you. When you choose not to judge others, God chooses to also not judge you.

➤ It robs you of good relationships

People who walk in unforgiveness cut themselves off from others. They rob themselves of meaningful relationships. Many times you'll hear an unforgiving person saying, "I don't want a woman or a man in my life again. I got hurt and I don't trust people anymore. I will never get married." At the bottom of those comments we will often find unforgiveness. You have to forgive and let go. There are wonderful relationships awaiting you behind the curtain of forgiveness.

➤ It divides families

There are many families who are divided over an inheritance. Some have parted ways because of a small house, yet they are staying in bigger houses. If you have to listen to the stories that divide some families, you would not believe it. You will hear that one family member made a comment without knowledge at a funeral and the family was divided. When you listen to it you find it's the pettiest of issues.

➤ Unforgiveness makes adults look like fools

Unforgiveness is the most foolish thing. It causes two adults passing each other act like they don't see one another. You see the person coming this way, but you look the other way as if you don't see them. That is a foolish game to play, especially for an adult. Even small children don't play that game. They forgive and forget easily.

➤ Unforgiveness clouds your judgement

A person who is walking in unforgiveness cannot judge things well when a person they have not forgiven is involved. They will say, "I will not go if she is there. I will not buy this if she is selling it." Meanwhile they can get it the cheapest from that person. They will say, "I will not eat this food if she cooked it," meanwhile they are hungry. Don't let unforgiveness and pride cloud your judgement.

➢ Unforgiveness makes you ugly

A person with an unforgiving spirit continuously pulls their face. They walk with a frown and a pouted mouth the whole day. You disfigure your face to scare off someone else, but you end up looking ugly.

➢ It steals your joy

A person who walks in unforgiveness does not have joy. They do not enjoy their life. Other people will be happy and enjoying themselves and they will sit there sour and bitter. Everybody else will be enjoying the conversation and laughing at light jokes, but they will suppress their emotions to punish the other person.

➢ It makes your world small

Unforgiveness makes you avoid places where you might meet a person to whom you are walking in unforgiveness.

➢ It denies you access to people you need

You will hear many people say in a meeting, "That person can help us but the two of us are not on speaking terms." I had a guy who was doing some work on my car and I told him I needed my car to be buffed and polished. He told me that the only person he knew who is good was his brother, but they were not on speaking terms. They had an argument over his brother and his wife staying with his mm and not helping with the expenses.

I went to his brother and told him, "Man, your brother is talking good things about you. He says you are the best when it comes to buffing and polishing a car." He smiled politely and said, "You know, we are not even talking to one another." I asked why and he told me the story. I said, "Your brother told me the same story and it looks like he wants to make peace with you." I saw relief on his face.

A few months later I needed his brother's services again and when I walked into the workshop I saw him and said, "Are you back?" He said, "Yes Pastor, we cleared our differences." I was so happy for them. His brother's business suffered because he could not offer buffing because the two of them were not on talking terms. He also suffered because his brother had an existing clientele from whom he could make money on a daily basis instead of sitting at home waiting for referrals and having to go to people's homes. He was now stationed in a proper workshop and he could make money.

Unforgiveness will deny you access to people you need. The sooner you forgive, the better your life will be. You might be suffering in your business, personal life, family or workplace right now because of unforgiveness. Just let it go and forgive.

Why we should forgive

➢ So God can forgive you

Matthew 6:14-15 NKJV
[14] For if you forgive men their trespasses, your heavenly Father will also forgive you. [15] But if you do not forgive men their trespasses, neither will your Father forgive your trespasses.

When you forgive others, God forgives you.

➢ To release yourself from bondage

When you are walking in unforgiveness you are punishing yourself. You are not punishing the other person. You are walking in bondage and making your own world small. A bitter person ignorantly thinks they are punishing the person who disappointed them. They will be pulling their face and be sour while the other person is laughing and joking with others. They will be thinking, "Look at him, this ugly thing, look how he is laughing." That is self-punishment.

➤ To free yourself from the judgement of God

If you are walking in unforgiveness you bring judgement on yourself. Your unforgiveness determines the judgement God should use toward you. When you do not forgive others, God will not forgive you.

➤ To give God a chance to judge the matter

Romans 12:19-21 NIV
[19] Do not take revenge, my friends, but leave room for God's wrath, for it is written: "It is mine to avenge; I will repay," says the Lord. [20] On the contrary: "If your enemy is hungry, feed him; if he is thirsty, give him something to drink. In doing this, you will heap burning coals on his head." [21] Do not be overcome by evil, but overcome evil with good.

Many people think they are better than God. They think their punishment to their enemies is better than God's punishment. They feel God is not capable of judging others. They feel God is too soft. They feel they are better judges than God. Such a person is equal to the antichrist because they feel they can do better than God. When you forgive your enemy, the Bible says you heap more coals on his head. Give the matter to God; He is a fair judge and much more powerful than you.

➤ Unforgiveness can make you sick

A person who walks in unforgiveness is bitter in their soul. They are full of fury. People who are bitter in their souls are more likely to attract cancers and depression. They are constantly walking in bitterness. They are rarely happy.

Why some people find it hard to forgive

➢ They feel they have been wronged greatly

We can never downplay the fact that you may have been greatly hurt. Most people who find it hard to forgive do so because they have been terribly wronged. But to carry a person in your heart and be bitter toward them does not punish them; it punishes you. I think it would be unfair to still punish yourself after you have been hurt so greatly.

➢ They feel they have done nothing wrong

Most of the time people who refuse to forgive others feel that they are not the person who has done something wrong. They feel the other person was wrong and that person should ask forgiveness. Jesus said if you bring your gift to the altar and your brother has something against you, you should leave your gift there and go and make right with your brother.

Many times you might find that a person was sexually abused, and yes, they have done nothing wrong. The other person is one hundred percent wrong. But when you become unforgiving, that's when you start doing something wrong. Forgiveness does not necessarily mean you do not make a case. It means you choose to let go of the resentment and bitterness toward the person. You let go of your anger.

Matthew 5:23-24 NKJV
[23] Therefore if you bring your gift to the altar, and there remember that your brother has something against you, [24] leave your gift there before the altar and go your way. First be reconciled to your brother, and then come and offer your gift.

➤ They feel nobody will understand how the person has hurt them

Nobody will ever experience a hurt the way you have experienced it, and you will also never experience the same hurt the way somebody else experienced it. The truth is that most of us, if not all of us in the world, have been hurt before and we all had to forgive.

➤ They feel the person has gone too far

We probably all have different levels of things that might be right and acceptable, or unacceptable, to us in our relationships. That is right, because we all need principles that govern our engagements and interactions with others. When your principles destroy good relationships around you, it can either be that your principles are unpratical or that you are unforgiving.

➤ They feel they have to protect themselves

Nobody wants to travel a road on which they know there are dangers that have caused them pain before. You don't have to sit on the lap of someone that has hurt you, but you can at least walk in forgiveness toward them.

➤ They feel if they forgive the person the person will do it again

Remember Jesus said you have to forgive someone seventy times seven times per day when they sin against you. That is four hundred and ninety times in one day. Has the person you are refusing to forgive offended you four hundred and ninety-one times in one day?

➤ They think too much of themselves

Don't let your pride be the barrier toward your forgiveness.

➢ They are naive in thinking nobody is ever going to offend them

Maybe I need to remind you – this is planet earth. If you are going to choose to live among the human species, you are going to need to include forgiveness in your life package.

➢ They are bitter in the soul

Choose to be sweet and tender-hearted. Don't make your life a nightmare train ride. Choose to see the good side of people.

➢ They forget how they needed forgiveness

When others do you wrong, think back on how God has forgiven you.

➢ They are too proud

Many people are too proud to humble themselves and ask forgiveness from another person. Their pride just won't allow them to do it. We read in **James 4:6** *"God resists the proud, But gives grace to the humble."*

➢ They feel the person did it on purpose

It is true that someone may have hurt you on purpose and they might not be truly sorry for what they have done. Carrying them in your heart will weigh you down. Just let it go.

➢ They are just unreasonable

There are people who are just plainly unreasonable. If a person corrects them, they will say, "I know I am wrong, but I don't need her to come and tell me. Who does she think she is?" I was puzzled to learn that two family members were not talking to each other for years because the one just told the other, "You have to contribute toward the household. You can't just let my mother spend all her pension on you and your girlfriend." I think you must be unreasonable to think your brother has done you wrong by trying to help you be responsible.

The benefits of forgiveness

➤ You feel free

Most people who have forgiven others feel like a weight has been taken off their shoulders. You don't know the burden of unforgiveness until you forgive.

➤ You feel happier

People who forgive others are happier. They feel more joyful. Bitterness makes the world look dull and colourless.

➤ Your world is bigger

Your world becomes bigger when you forgive others. You can suddenly go anywhere. You can visit the person whom you have forgiven.

➤ You feel connected

When you forgive others you suddenly feel more connected. People who forgive others often feel like they want to do something together with that person. A family member might feel to go somewhere together as a family. It is the inherent need of a human being to connect with others.

How to forgive

The act of forgiveness is the easiest thing, but it can be the hardest to do. You don't have to wait for a special inspiration to forgive someone. You just got to do it.

➢ You can just send a message

Sometimes all it takes for you to forgive someone is to send a message saying, "Please forgive me," or "I forgive you." That depends on your relationship with the person. Some people will take offence if you send them a message. You have to do what will work for your relationship.

Make a phone call
A phone call can make a world's difference. When you call, just to hear the person's voice can make a difference. Don't hesitate to make the call and tell someone you forgive them.

➢ Call a meeting

A meeting can be one of the most challenging things, but because of the nature of your challenge it would be appropriate to call a meeting.

➢ Bump into the person

Sometimes it is best to position yourself to just bump into the person in the passage or on the road and reach out to them.

➢ Do it for you

When you go out to forgive, do it for your own sake and not so much for the sake of the other person. If they don't respond favourably, don't say, "You see, that is why I don't want to forgive him or her. I knew she would act this way." Let the person act anyway they like. Don't be moved. Be aware that God sees it all. He will judge the case.

➢ Be the least

Even if you were right, be the least. Don't say, "She better keep quiet because she was the one who started it." Be forgiving. Don't be judgemental when you forgive.

➢ Admit your wrong

When you are asking forgiveness, the person might have interpreted you in a wrong way. This is not the time to try and correct or defend yourself. Just tell them, "I did not mean to hurt you, but I have hurt you and for that I am sorry." Don't be vague by saying, "If I have hurt or offended you, please forgive me." That means you do not admit you were wrong. Be specific and ask forgiveness for having hurt the person.

➢ Repent before God

If you have walked in unforgiveness, repent before God and ask for His forgiveness.

➢ Receive forgiveness if the person has already died

If the person to whom you are walking in bitterness has already died, you can receive forgiveness. The person would have forgiven you. Don't punish yourself any longer. Just repent before God and ask Him to forgive you.

Make every effort to walk in forgiveness

Make an effort to live in peace with everyone in your relationships. Make no room for bitterness and unforgiveness.

Hebrews 12:14-15 NIV
[14] Make every effort to live in peace with everyone and to be holy; without holiness no one will see the Lord. [15] See to it that no one falls short of the grace of God and that no bitter root grows up to cause trouble and defile many.

OTHER BOOKS BY PASTOR GERALD HUGO

ABOUT THE BOOK

Being a Christian does not automatically relate to being victorious and successful. Your success and victory are determined by your faith in God. Your faith is determined by your belief system. If your belief system does not make room for prosperity, you will not have the faith to trust God for financial abundance. If your belief system does not make room for miracles, you will not be able to believe God for divine healing. Your belief system is formed by the teaching you receive.

In this book you will learn:

- How to respond to the storms of life.
- The truth about bloodline and family curses.
- How to live the Blessed Life.
- Is tithing Law or Grace?
- How you can receive complete healing.
- The truth about Deliverance.
- Why the world loves God, but they reject Jesus.
- The purpose of the Holy Spirit in your Life.

Pastor Hugo is the senior Pastor and founder of Grace Tabernacle Church, and author of the famous *Power on Demand Daily Devotions* that are read by people around the world on social media and in book format. He is also the author of the bestselling book *How to Interpret your Dreams and Visions*, a book that helps people to interpret their own dreams and visions, with a dream dictionary of over one hundred pages. He is the host of the weekly television broadcast *Power on Demand* that airs on various television channels and online.